## Dedication

I would like to dedicate this book to my mother. She was the queen of saving scraps. She was the queen of saving everything, but particularly things with relevance to sewing. She saved countless zippers, buttons, fabric scraps, and patterns. She taught us the importance of appreciating the things you have, and she was "green" before recycling and green technology were ever considered.

My mother was always there to give an encouraging word or a helping hand. She knew just when to tell us to rip something out and when to hold back and let us experiment, lest we lose our enthusiasm.

She has long since passed away. Her words reverberate in my head every day when I am at my sewing machine or cutting something out. "Don't cut right in the center of that fabric," or "Make sure you watch that seam allowance," were words that we lived by.

Thanks, Mom, for all the hard work and the encouragement to pursue something with such timelessness.

## Acknowledgments

At the risk of seeming trite, I would like to say thank you to my husband and family. Husbands and families of quilters and sewists are really an impressive lot. They have to be okay with minimalist dinners. They have to be okay with not having a perfectly clean house. They have to be okay with dishes stacked in the sink and with more quilts in the linen closet than clean towels.

My husband and family are just that—impressive. They are more than okay with all of my shortcomings because they appreciate my passions. Either that or they realize that if I get to sew, I will be infinitely happier, and therefore the day will go more smoothly.

As of this book, I am an empty nester. Well, not quite completely. My son is our youngest child, and he is in college. Our children still come home a great deal but never permanently. So my life has changed, and I now have even more time to sew.

So thank you, family. You have given me the gift of being able to pursue my goal of writing a book or two. Love you!

# CONTENTS

## PROJECTS

The Windows in My Baby's Room 21

Aromatic Rings 26

Packages, Boxes, and Bows 31

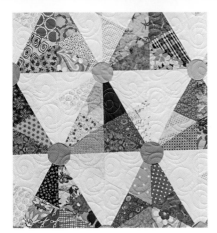

The Circus Comes to Town 37

Blended Hexagons 43

Star Baby 50

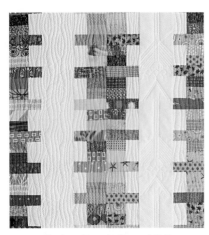

Color Brick Road 57

Owl's Well That Ends Well 63

William Tell 70

Clinging Vine 80

Rectangles Squared 84

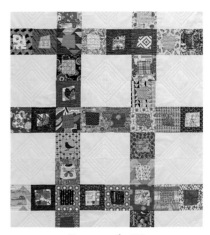

Fretwork 90

# INTRODUCTION

Every single quilt in this book uses nothing more than 3½", 4½", and/or 5½" squares. That's right. This combination is magical. This is the second of my two books that take this approach to quiltmaking.

I was a frustrated quilter. Each time I looked at a book about scrap quilting, I found that it was written from the perspective of using precuts or new pieces of fabric cut into strips. While the resulting quilts were beautiful, they didn't fit the bill for me. I had so many scraps that I wanted to use in an organized, meaningful way. So while playing in my sewing room, I came up with a different system. Following this system, I used only squares in the sizes mentioned above and the scraps in my bins to create all of the quilts that you see in this book.

Welcome to the first day of the rest of your piece-of-scrap life! Yes, I said "piece-of-scrap." To a quilter or a sewist, that's a good thing!

Do you have lots of scraps? Most of us do. We have fabric left over from making garments, making bags, making other quilts—and, of course, fabric given to us by people who know we love fabric. Those well-meaning friends and acquaintances drop fabric at our door, knowing that we just can't resist taking a peek.

With this book, I intend to help you. I'll help you sort your scraps, and I'll help you to see that you don't need to buy new fabric to create beautiful scrap quilts. All the fabric you need is right there at your fingertips.

> **Note:** *You can change the size of many of the quilts in this book by reducing the number of blocks (to make the quilt smaller) or increasing the number of blocks (to make the quilt larger).*

So grab your favorite chair, plop yourself down, and start reading!

## Do You Have a Sprite?

The sprite has been busy!

In all of our sewing rooms lives a sprite. She is lively, loves color, and has an aversion to discarding things that have meaning and are beautiful. Late at night, when most sewists are sound asleep, she rummages through the colorful scraps in the sewing room and duplicates them. They begin to multiply. Eventually they take over the room.

She doesn't complete her work in a single night— oh, no. It takes some time. If she did this in a single night, it would become evident too quickly to the sewist in the house. The sprite must go about her work cautiously so as not to be found out.

It's the only explanation. Surely no one in her right mind would have such a huge collection of scraps. But, alas, we do. Most of the scraps are irregular in shape and size and can't be used for strip quilting.

These scraps are large enough to be put to good use, but they are not conducive to strip quilting.

So what's a quilter to do? Get rid of the sprite? Or use up the scraps? Well, obviously, use up the scraps.

We sew bags; we sew hats. We sew garments. And lately we've been sewing umbrellas. These give you odd-shaped scraps. But boy, do we ever have fun making them. Many of our customers want to make them, too. As a result, we have many odd scraps that need to find a home.

In the photo above, you can see that the circles cut for these hats and their brims would leave you with odd-shaped scraps.

# Options for Cutting Scraps

All of the quilt projects in this book are made by cutting 3½", 4½", or 5½" squares. This can be accomplished in any of three ways.

- You can use my fast2cut Simple Square Templates (by C&T Publishing).

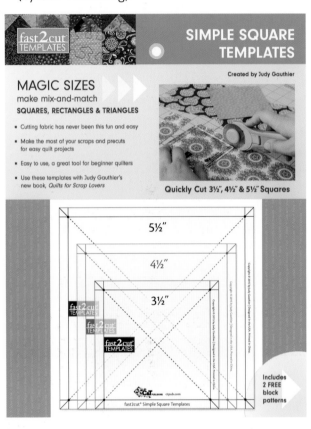

- You can mark a standard rotary cutting ruler using masking tape or my Tear-Perfect Maker Tape (by C&T Publishing).

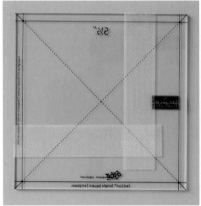

> **Note:** *My Tear-Perfect Maker Tape (by C&T Publishing) is a great new tape that can be applied to acrylic templates or rulers. It is scored throughout on a grid, so it tears exactly where you want it to. You can apply it to a ruler and leave it on for months with no residue when it is removed. And it releases so much more easily than masking tape.*
>
> *When you use Tear-Perfect Maker Tape to mark a measurement on a ruler or template, the ridge butts up against the edge of the fabric, giving you a perfect measurement. And it keeps the ruler or template from sliding.*

- You can cut using an unmarked standard rotary cutting ruler.

# Using Scraps

You may ask, how do you create a quilt with fabric that comes from, well, all walks of life?

Some of us have lots of different kinds of fabric scraps. With my system of making scrap quilts, it doesn't matter what type of fabric you have. I guarantee that you can mix many of these fabrics even within the same quilt.

# How to "Space" for the Best Use of Odd Fabrics

Spacing is essential when using fabrics that would otherwise clash. Many people refer to this as *balance* rather than spacing. I like the term *spacing* because balance can be a more subjective concept, whereas spacing usually involves straightforward instructions on how many "blanks" to use between colored fabrics.

When I refer to "blanks," I mean blocks that are constructed in the same way as other blocks but using neutral colors. Spacing can also be achieved by using a solid square that is not pieced between the pieced blocks.

As a quilter you have fabrics in your scrap bins that you think could never be used together. Let me assure you that with a little spacing help, they can be used together effectively.

Many of you have neutral "background" fabrics you have collected over the years. Creating a unit or block using these fabrics between the colorful blocks makes for an interesting quilt, and it allows you to use difficult-to-match fabrics within the blocks.

Spacing the colorful fabrics by putting a neutral block between them keeps them from "fighting."

- - - - - - - - - - - - - - - - - - - - - - - - - - - - - - - - - - - - - - - - - -

# Understanding Intensity Creates Great Results

I think intensity (or *value*: light, medium, and dark) is more important than color.

Many quilters are very anxious when it comes to color selection. For most of my quilts, I have not agonized too much about color selection. That's because in order to use up as many scraps as possible, you can't worry as much about color. You want to use as many scraps as you can, so you are mainly going to be looking at the degree of contrast among your scraps. A good scrap quilt will have a balance of lights, mediums, and darks.

My best piece of advice with regard to intensity is to take a photo of your scraps using the black-and-white feature on your camera. (Most cameras have this feature, and all smart phones do.) When you look at a photo of a stack of scraps, you should see a variety of lights, mediums, and darks. If you don't, you will need to adjust your scrap selection to achieve the most successful results.

This stack of fabrics has a good combination of lights, mediums, and darks.

Color is almost secondary to light, medium, and dark intensity. See how well these work together when the color is hidden?

# ORGANIZING YOUR FABRICS

Organizing your fabrics will make it a million times easier to choose fabrics for the best possible scrap quilts. There are many ways to organize your fabrics. My personal preference is by color.

> **Note:** *When I am actually in the selection process for a quilt, I also divide fabrics into light and dark, and warm and cool.*

Find a space that will accommodate shelving, ideally with cubbies, so each color can have a separate spot. If you can't build cubbies, you can also use baskets or boxes. Make sure they are stored out of direct sunlight, because sunlight will damage your fabric considerably.

> **TIP** *Having your fabrics out where you can see them is a good way to save money. I don't know about you, but with me it's "out of sight, out of mind." If I don't see a fabric, I will forget I have it—so it won't get used, and I'll buy more.*

> **Note:** *In order to be put into a cubby, a piece of fabric must be ½ yard or larger in size.*

I separate my fabrics first by color: red, orange, yellow, gold, brown, green, turquoise/aqua, blue, pink, purple, white, black, and tan (which is good for backgrounds and is understated). Halloween and Christmas have their own cubbies.

If you are uncertain about how to classify a fabric because of the multitude of colors in it, look at the background color. If this doesn't help, then create a cubby for fabrics that have such a multitude of colors that they cannot be defined. These fabrics are called the "I don't know what you are, but I love you anyway" fabrics. I think this is a good metaphor for life!

My cubby system spans floor to ceiling.

> **Note:** *If a fabric is larger than ½ yard and has a little bit cut from it, I will try to fold it so there aren't any selvage pieces or other stray pieces hanging from it. The cubby system is much more aesthetically pleasing that way. But as long as a fabric piece is larger than ½ yard, it stays on the shelf.*

I have a wire drawer system for fat quarters. Wire drawers may be purchased at big-box do-it-yourself stores. You can see your fabric, and each drawer is sorted by color.

Next come the scraps. They're the ones we loved before we used them, loved as we used them, and still love even though they're not perfect.

I store my fun, less-than-perfectly shaped scraps (leftover strips from jelly rolls, pieces from charm packs, and scraps) in tubs. Yes, tubs. I use transparent ones so I can see what is in them. I have a tub for each of the colors for which I have a cubby.

If you follow my system, you probably won't have a lot of room left at this stage. We've talked about cubbies, wire drawers, and now tubs. And you still need to have room for your sewing machine! So you are going to need to stack those tubs, and they can get heavy.

Here is the last step in the organizational system. Tape bags to the edge of your sewing table or cutting table. Why would you ever do that? Well, if you're like me, you won't want to stop every time you create a scrap. You will pile them up on your cutting table until you're good and ready to throw them into the correct bin. Instead, tape a couple of bags to your cutting table or sewing table. When you have a scrap, throw it into one of the bags. Then, once a week, put the scraps in the correct bins.

Whew! That was a lot of information, but now you can have some fun choosing fabrics!

# CHOOSING FABRICS FOR SCRAP QUILTS

Many people think that to make a scrap quilt you must use an assortment of all the scraps you own. Not true! You can decide on a theme or color scheme beforehand, and then pick your fabrics accordingly. Just because it's a scrap quilt doesn't mean that it has to be devoid of a theme.

For the most part, you are going to be picking from your bins. The entire premise of this book is to help you use up your odd scraps—but that doesn't mean that you can't add a few new fabric pieces here and there if they are a good fit.

Decide what feeling you want your quilt to convey. Do you want a scrappy holiday feeling?

A summer theme of new shoots and blossoms

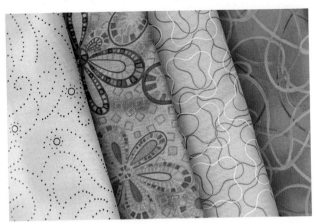

A more citrusy, summery feeling

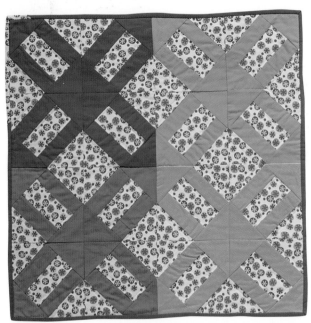

*Holiday Scrap Crackers* features a pattern from my book *Quilts for Scrap Lovers* (by C&T Publishing). The tabletop quilt's candy motif and solids were left over from making Christmas pajamas.

Perhaps you are trying to convey a summery look. Will it be reflective of the greenery of summer foliage or have a beachy or citrusy feeling?

A woodsy feeling

**TIP** *If you have lots of scraps and want to work using a very specific color scheme, you can refer to one of the many products on the market, such as the color tools from Joen Wolfrom (by C&T Publishing).*

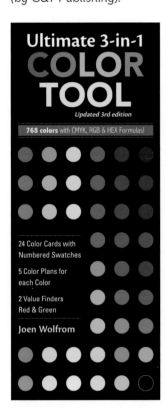

# Warm and Cool Colors

Although many people equate warm and cool colors with intensity, this is not an accurate association. Warm and cool colors have less to do with intensity than they do with mood. If you look at the color wheel, you will see that the warm colors tend to be on one side of the color wheel and the cool colors on the other.

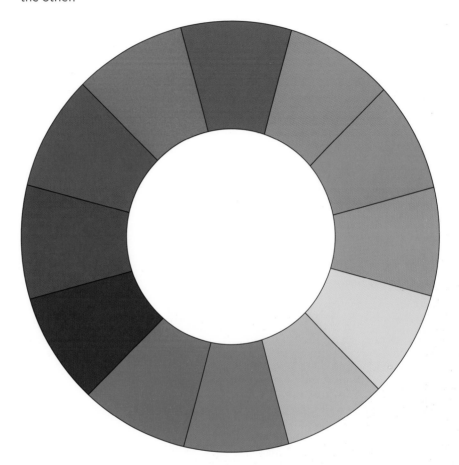

When I am referencing warm colors, I am talking about anything from yellow over to red. The cool colors are on the other side of the color wheel, and I am speaking now of green through blue.

There are a couple of colors that are generally in between, and these are purples that lean more toward the red end of the spectrum and greens that lean more toward the yellow end of the spectrum.

The effects of color may be simplified by saying that the warm colors charge our emotions. They make us feel comfortable, and well, warm. Red is a great color for marketing: It tends to make us feel good even though it may not be our favorite color. Cool tones are calming and restful. Most people think these are the colors that should be found in bedrooms or in quiet, restful spots.

So what does all this have to do with quilting?

Warm and cool tones evoke certain feelings. Your choice will depend on what your quilt is trying to convey. Look at the pile of fabric shown below. The fabrics all have warm tones, with an ambiguous one thrown in. How does it look to you? Playful? Bold? Youthful?

This fabric grouping has a definite look and feel to it.

Now look at this next grouping. It certainly feels different than the previous one.

This colorway may be more appropriate in a room that feels restful.

Remember, not all quilts are made as bed quilts. Many are wall art, and art is definitely meant to convey certain feelings.

Now, having said that, I have to mention one little thing: Unless you are definitely trying to convey a sentiment with the color scheme or are doing it as a request, don't make a quilt to match a paint color or the color scheme of a room. *What?* I can hear all the commotion coming from readers! Think about this. All quilts are art. When you purchase a work of art, do you buy it because it matches the room? Not usually. Most people purchase art because it moves them.

I tell you this because it will free up your spirit to take a chance. Use that fabric you love. Use a fabric that moves you. Being a quilt shop owner, I often see people buy a piece of fabric and say, "I don't know what I am going to do with it, but I just love it!" Those are the greatest words a shop owner can hear, because you know you have reached someone with a piece of your fabric. You have made a connection.

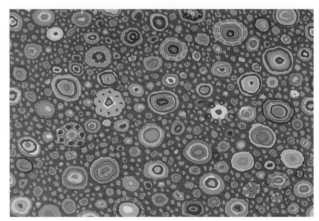

This is one of my most beloved pieces of fabric. I have cut it up and used it in many of my scrap quilts.

So put that fabric in—but help it to fit according to the rules of color, intensity, spacing, and possibly, theme.

# Finding Inspiration in Unusual Places

Many people forget to look at the world as a color palette. I like to do this because it brings me fresh inspiration for how to put fabrics together. Almost everyone has a cell phone with them at all times these days. So put yours to work for you. Create a folder for pictures you take that may give you color inspiration for your next quilt.

Take some trees with bright red berries, for example. The berries are juxtaposed with lovely brownish-gray branches. Take a picture! How about cereal boxes? The companies that make cereal have entire art departments devoted to the science of making things look good. Take advantage of this and take a picture. Or what about washing dishes? (A mundane task for certain.) I have Fiesta Dinnerware. While washing these bowls, it struck me: Look at what a great color combination this is! For decades Homer Laughlin (the producer of Fiesta Dinnerware) has been committed to the science of color.

Most of the quilts in this book contain random smatterings of my scraps, and they are built to accommodate as many scraps as possible. But there is one monochromatic quilt with a very planned-out color scheme: *Blended Hexagons*. For this quilt I really emptied out the orange and pink scrap bins.

Have fun playing with the fabric selections for each quilt. Many of them are monochromatic within an area, and this makes for easy decision making.

Finding color inspiration everywhere

*Aromatic Rings* (page 26) has a monochromatic theme within each individual block.

# Taking Print Scale into Consideration

I am one of those rare people who is totally undaunted by large-scale prints. Often people come into the shop, look at large-scale prints, and become terrified. We have had so many years of small little ditzy prints that large prints scare some quilters. If there's one bit of advice I usually give to people, it's not to be afraid to use the large-scale prints in the blocks of their quilts.

So many people look at a large-scale print and think that it can only be used in a border. Not so. I also hear the comment repeatedly, "I think that's too big to be used in that block. People won't know what it is." Well, let's challenge that theory.

When a quilter looks at the piece of fabric shown below, it looks like a scary large-scale print. It was very popular in my shop, and it sold quickly, but most of the customers admitted that they didn't know what they would do with it.

Most quilters might say that it would make a cute blouse, which it would. They might say that it would go well on the border of a quilt that had umbrellas in it. Yes, you could do that. But let's break this down.

Lay the 5½" template from the fast2cut Simple Square Templates (by C&T Publishing) or your rotary cutting ruler over the motif. Don't center it so that the characters are right in the middle. Place it so there are portions of the motif included in the square but not precisely in the center.

Now, if you cut out the square, look at the results.

Is there any question that the motif shows a man and woman with an umbrella? No. There's no question. It's not hitting you in the face like the well-centered picture of something that a child would draw, but it definitely leaves the viewer looking at it for more than just a split second. It draws the viewer in.

You don't necessarily have to center the motifs. Because they're scraps, they should be used to their best advantage as scraps. The quilter should cut over to the edge so as not to waste fabric. I can still hear my mother's words: "Don't cut right in the middle of that scrap!"

Here's a photo of a baby that is taken slightly off center. This is the same concept. Even though you can't see the entire baby in the photo, there's no question that it's a baby.

*Photo by Judy Gauthier*

# HALF-SQUARE TRIANGLES AND A FEW IMPORTANT NOTES

## ¼" Seam Allowances

All seam allowances used in this book are ¼".

It is very important to use a ¼" foot. If you don't have one, make sure to measure where the ¼" seam allowance is on your machine. You can do this by lifting your presser foot and slowly lowering your needle down onto a ruler on an inch marking. Look to see where the ¼" mark is from the needle, and mark this on your machine.

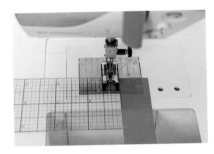

Once you have done this, make sure you always sew a ¼" seam allowance where indicated.

Test your seam allowance by cutting 2 pieces of fabric the same size. Sew them together with a ¼" seam allowance and press. Measure the sewn unit across the seam. It should be ½" smaller than the total width of the 2 pieces you cut. For instance, 2 pieces 2" wide sewn together with a ¼" seam should now measure 3½" wide.

Adjust your needle position or the marking on your machine until it is accurate.

- - - - - - - - - - - - - - - - - - - - - - - - - - - - - - - - - - - -

## Half-Square Triangles

When I refer to half-square triangle (HST) units, I am referring to an entire square that is made up of 2 triangles joined along their long edges. So 1 HST unit is 1 square, 2 HST units are 2 squares, and so on.

There are two ways to make half-square triangles for the quilts in this book.

### Method 1

This method creates 2 half-square triangles that frequently need to be squared down to a different size.

**1.** Place 2 contrasting squares of fabric right sides together.

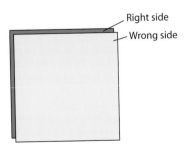

Right side
Wrong side

**2.** Draw a diagonal line on the top square from corner to corner, using a water-soluble pen and a ruler.

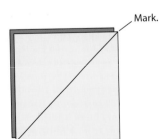

Mark.

**3.** Stitch ¼" on both sides of the diagonal line.

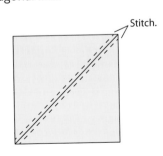

Stitch.

**4.** Cut on the diagonal line, using your rotary cutter or scissors.

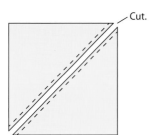

Cut.

**5.** Open up the triangles and press the seam allowance toward the darker fabric.

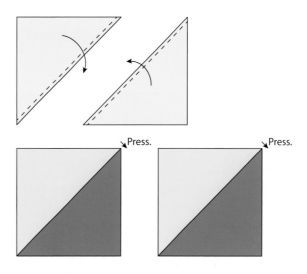

Press.     Press.

---

# Method 2

Method 2 creates a single half-square triangle unit. This square will measure the same size as the square that you started with.

This method leaves 2 unused snippets of fabric. Do not discard these. There are many fun quilts that you can make with them.

**1.** Place 2 contrasting squares of fabric right sides together.

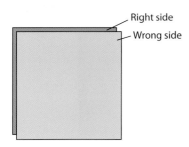

Right side
Wrong side

**2.** Draw a diagonal line on the top square from corner to corner, using a water-soluble pen and a ruler.

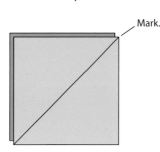

Mark.

**3.** Stitch directly on the drawn line.

**4.** Cut ¼" away from the stitching line on one side.

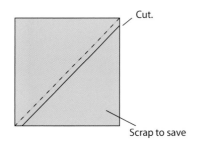

Cut.

Scrap to save

**5.** Press the seam allowance toward the darker fabric.

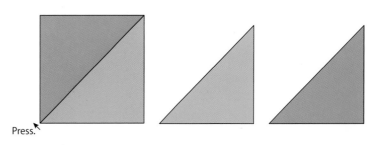

Press.

# How to Accurately Apply Borders

To measure an accurate border that isn't wavy, you should measure across the center of your quilt rather than along the quilt's edges. If the quilt was set aside for a period of time and the edges became stretched, or if they were stretched in the process of piecing the quilt top, the edges will be longer than the center of your quilt. If you add a border using the outer measurement, the border will appear wavy because it actually is larger than your inner measurement.

Measure the length of the quilt through the center of the quilt, from top to bottom. This will be the length to cut the side borders.

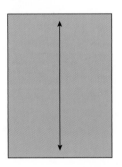

Cut the border strips in your desired width to the measured length, piecing the strips together if necessary. Stitch the side borders to the quilt top and press toward the borders.

Then measure through the center of the quilt from side to side, including the side borders. This is the length to cut the top and bottom borders.

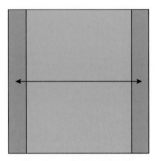

Cut the border strips in your desired width as measured, piecing the strips together if necessary. Stitch the top and bottom borders to the quilt top and press toward the borders.

- - - - - - - - - - - - - - - - - - - - - - - - - - - - - - - - - - - - - -

# Let's Get Going!

I hope this book will be useful and fun. We all have so many scraps we need to use up. This book gives you a plan for using them to make beautiful quilts.

# THE WINDOWS IN MY BABY'S ROOM

**FINISHED QUILT:** 52½" × 52½" · **FINISHED BLOCK:** 10" × 10"

This quilt uses the concepts of the very traditional Cathedral Windows block. It creates a curved piecing look without requiring you to sew curves. When you are choosing scraps, keep in mind that you will be pairing them up. Choose fabrics that contrast well but also look great together. Since you are only cutting two squares 5½″ × 5½″ from each scrap, you don't need very large scrap pieces.

## Materials

- 32 assorted larger scraps, each large enough to yield 2 squares 5½″ × 5½″
- 8 assorted smaller scraps, each large enough to yield 2 squares 3½″ × 3½″
- 2½ yards of solid white fabric for background and outer border
- ½ yard of contrasting fabric for inner border
- 61″ × 61″ backing
- 61″ × 61″ batting
- ½ yard for binding

## Cutting

See Options for Cutting Scraps (page 8).

### Larger scraps

- Cut 2 squares 5½″ × 5½″ from each fabric to total 64 squares.

### Smaller scraps

- Cut 2 squares 3½″ × 3½″ from each fabric to total 16 squares.

### White

- Cut 10 strips 5½″ × width of fabric; subcut 64 squares 5½″ × 5½″ for the background.
- Cut 5 strips 4½″ × width of fabric for the outer border.

### Contrasting fabric

- Cut 5 strips 2½″ × width of fabric for the inner border.

# Making the Mock Cathedral Window Blocks

*All seam allowances are ¼" unless otherwise stated.*

**1.** Match 1 pair of 5½" × 5½" squares with a second contrasting pair, right sides together, as shown.

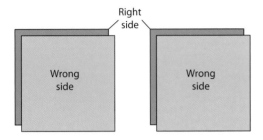

**2.** Using method 1 (page 18) and the paired 5½" × 5½" squares, make 4 half-square triangle (HST) units.

**3.** Fold each HST unit as shown, wrong sides together; align the seam. Press the fold with a hot iron.

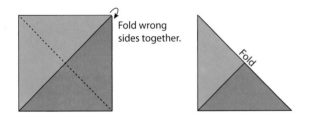

**4.** Place the folded HST unit on the bottom left corner of a right-side-up background square, as shown. Pin along the raw edges on the sides.

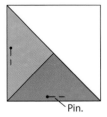

**5.** Starting ¼" from the corner, roll the folded edge of the HST unit back onto itself. The roll should be about ⅜" wide. Leave the last ¼" unrolled. Pin this roll.

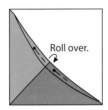

**6.** Stitch the curved edge of the roll through all thicknesses, backstitching for 1 or 2 stitches at the beginning and end.

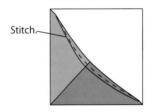

**7.** Trim off the piece of the HST unit that is underneath (the middle layer).

**8.** Repeat Steps 4–7 to make 4 identical units.

**9.** Arrange the 4 units in 2 rows of 2, rotating the units as needed to create a pinwheel design.

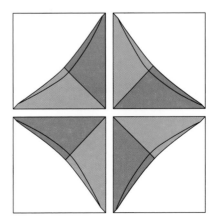

**10.** Sew the units together to make a block. Press the seam allowances in opposite directions so they will nest.

**11.** Repeat Steps 1–10 to make a total of 16 blocks.

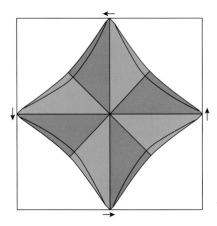

- - - - - - - - - - - - - - - - - - - - - - - - - - - - - - - - - - - - - - - - -

# Making and Attaching the Small Pinwheels

**1.** Follow Making the Mock Cathedral Window Blocks, Steps 1–3 (page 23), using the 3½″ × 3½″ squares to make 4 sets of 4 small folded HST units.

**2.** Refer to the quilt assembly diagram (next page) to lay out the Mock Cathedral Window blocks in a 4 × 4 layout.

**3.** Starting with the upper left-hand block, pin 1 small folded HST unit in 1 inner corner of each of 4 blocks, as shown, to make a pinwheel design.

**4.** Follow Making the Mock Cathedral Window Blocks, Steps 5–7 (page 23) to roll and stitch the folded edges of the small HST units to the block corners.

**5.** Repeat Steps 3 and 4 to make and attach 3 more sets of small HST units.

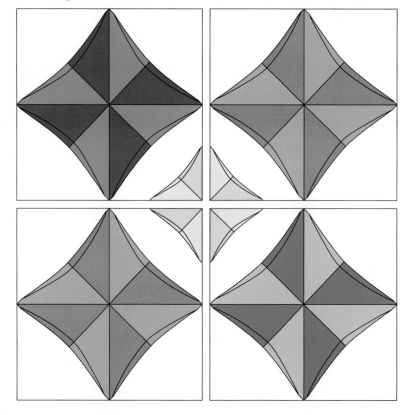

# Putting It All Together

*Refer to the arrows for pressing direction.*

**1.** Refer to the quilt assembly diagram (below) to stitch the Mock Cathedral Window blocks together in 4-block sections as shown, making sure you are matching the seams and corners with the small inner pinwheels. Press.

**2.** Stitch the 4-block sections together into 2 rows. Press.

**3.** Sew the 2 rows together. Press.

# Adding the Borders

Follow How to Accurately Apply Borders (page 20) to add the inner and outer borders.

# Finishing

Layer, baste, quilt, and bind as desired.

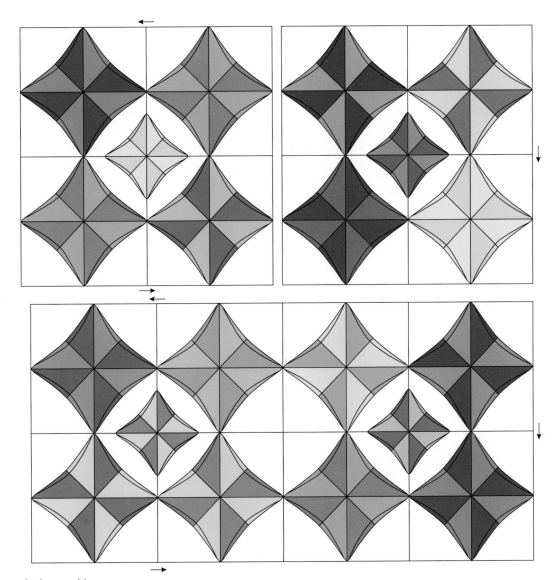

Quilt assembly

# AROMATIC RINGS

**FINISHED QUILT:** 75½" × 75½" • **FINISHED BLOCK:** 25" × 25"

*The basic shape of the unit for this quilt is somewhat like an elongated hexagon. When put together to form a ring, it reminds me very much of chemistry class.*

*I chose to make each block a different color. There is enough spacing between and around each hexagon to use a lot of different fabrics. This is a great design for using up some of those more difficult fabrics. You can also mix large- and small-scale prints with ease.*

*Each large block is composed of 25 background squares 5½″ × 5½″. Since the background squares are also scraps, it's a good way to use up the light-colored scraps you have in your stash.*

## Materials

- 9 groupings of 16 colored scraps in different colorways, each large enough to yield a 5½″ × 5½″ square (144 total)

- 225 assorted light scraps, each large enough to yield a 5½″ × 5½″ square

- 84″ × 84″ backing

- 84″ × 84″ batting

- ¾ yard for binding

## Cutting

*See Options for Cutting Scraps (page 8).*

Colored scraps

From each grouping:

- Cut 16 squares 5½″ × 5½″ (144 total).

Light scraps

- Cut 225 squares 5½″ × 5½″.

# Making the Hexagon Rings

*All seam allowances are ¼″.*

**1.** With a marking pen, mark 1⅛″ in from the top right and left corners of a colored 5½″ × 5½″ square.

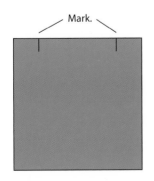
Mark.

**2.** Line up a ruler from one mark to the lower corner on the same side of the square. Cut with a rotary cutter. Repeat on the opposite side to create a tumbler shape.

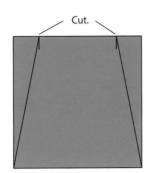
Cut.

**3.** Fold the tumbler in half, right sides together, along the long side. Press lightly so there is a center crease. Do not use spray starch or press heavily. You will be ironing out this fold line later.

Fold in half.

**4.** Stitch across the top and bottom. Trim off the corners along the fold.

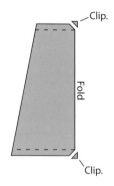

Clip.

Fold

Clip.

**TIP** *You can chainstitch these pieces and cut them apart when finished.*

**5.** Turn the tumbler right side out and use a bodkin, chopstick, or knitting needle to make a sharp point.

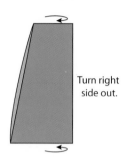

Turn right side out.

**6.** Match the seam allowance on the top and bottom to the center crease by pulling the seams down to the wrong side of the unit.

**7.** Press, eliminating the center crease and creating sharp creases and points at the top and bottom to a make an irregular hexagon.

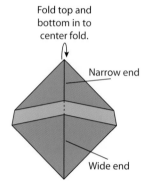

Fold top and bottom in to center fold.

Narrow end

Wide end

- - - - - - - - - - - - - - - - - - - - - - - - - - - - - - - - - - - - - - - - -

**8.** Repeat Steps 1–7 to make 16 hexagons for each of the 9 color groupings.

**9.** Join all 16 hexagons from 1 color grouping together in a ring. The narrow ends will be toward the center and the wide ends will be on the outside of the ring. Press the seam allowances open or to one side.

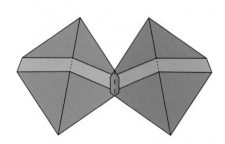

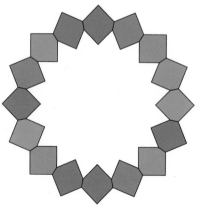

**10.** Repeat Step 9 to make a total of 9 hexagon rings.

# Making the Block Backgrounds

*Follow the arrows for pressing direction.*

1. Using the light 5½" × 5½" squares, sew 5 rows of 5 squares together. Press.

2. Join the rows together, matching seam allowances. Press.

3. Repeat Steps 1 and 2 to make a total of 9 block backgrounds.

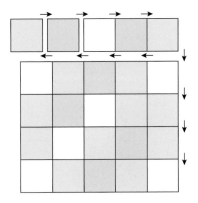

- - - - - - - - - - - - - - - - - - - - - - - - - - - - - - - - - - - - - - -

# Putting It All Together

1. Place a hexagon ring on top of a block background, centering it and making certain that it lays flat.

2. Pin or baste in place.

3. Using your preferred method of appliqué, sew the hexagon ring to the block background.

4. Repeat Steps 1–3 for all 9 blocks.

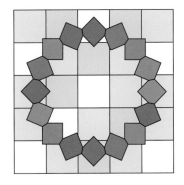

**TIP** *For this quilt, I machine stitched along the edges of both the outside and the inside of the ring. You could hand appliqué or machine appliqué in whatever fashion you desire.*

5. Refer to the quilt assembly diagram (page 30) to lay the blocks out in a 3 × 3 layout, rotating them so the seams will nest.

6. Sew the blocks into rows. Press.

7. Sew the rows together. Press the seam allowances all in the same direction.

# Finishing

Layer, baste, quilt, and bind as desired.

Quilt assembly

# PACKAGES, BOXES, AND BOWS

**FINISHED QUILT:** 80½″ × 80½″ • **FINISHED BLOCK:** 8″ × 8″

This quilt demonstrates why it is important to separate your odd-shaped scraps by color. I was able to go through the bins and create this progression. It was really fun revisiting all of the scraps. Choosing scraps for this quilt would be a great exercise for students, because it makes the quilter look carefully at which direction a color leans. When you pick a yellow out of the yellow bin, you need to look to see whether it leans toward orange or toward green. Or is it a pure yellow? The same may be said for the purples. Some purples definitely have more blue in them, and some have more red. It is a great exercise in color!

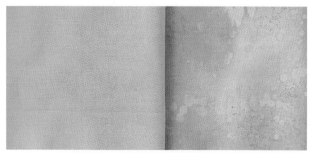

The yellow piece on the left definitely leans more toward green, while the one on the right leans more toward orange.

It's easy to see that the purple fabric on the left leans more toward red than the one on the right, which leans more toward blue.

---

## Materials

- 81 assorted scraps, each large enough to yield 3 squares 5½" × 5½"

- 6⅝ yards of white

- 89" × 89" backing

- 89" × 89" batting

- ¾ yard for binding

## Cutting

See Options for Cutting Scraps (page 8).

### Scraps

- Cut 3 squares 5½" × 5½" from each scrap (243 total).

### White

- Cut 35 strips 5½" × width of fabric; subcut 243 squares 5½" × 5½" for the blocks.

- Cut 8 strips 4½" × width of fabric for the borders.

### Cutting the bow ties

**1.** Layer 2 white 5½" × 5½" squares with 2 colored 5½" × 5½" squares.

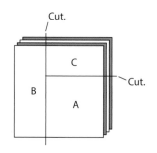

**2.** Cut the stack into 4 rectangles 5½" × 2" (B), 4 squares 3½" × 3½" (A), and 4 rectangles 3½" × 2" (C).

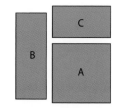

**Note:** Set aside the colored B and C rectangles for another project. They are leftovers.

Label the pieces A, B, and C, if desired.

# Making the Bow Tie End Units

*All seam allowances are ¼". Refer to the arrows for pressing direction.*

For each block:

**1.** Stitch a white C rectangle to a colored A square, right sides together. Press.

**2.** Repeat Step 1 to make a second matching A/C unit.

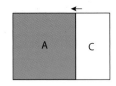

**3.** Stitch a white B rectangle to an A/C unit, right sides together. Press.

**4.** Repeat Step 3 with the second matching unit.

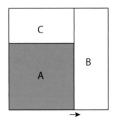

**5.** Trim both units to 4½" × 4½", trimming off the excess background fabric.

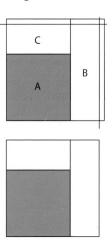

- - - - - - - - - - - - - - - - - - - - - - - - - - - - - - - - - - - - - - - - - - - -

# Making the Striped Units

For each block:

**1.** Use 1 white 5½" × 5½" square and 1 colored 5½" × 5½" square to create 2 half-square triangle (HST) units using method 1 (page 18).

**2.** Press the seam allowances as shown.

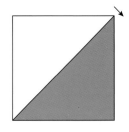

**3.** Lay a white A square over the colored half of 1 HST unit, matching the corners.

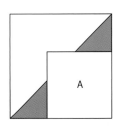

**4.** Draw a diagonal line across the white A square, as shown. Stitch directly on the drawn line. Trim ¼" away from the stitching line. *Do not discard the colored snippet—it will be added to the other side of the striped unit.*

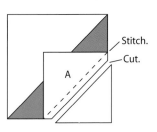

**5.** Press the seam allowance.

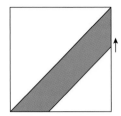

**6.** Lay the colored snippet from Step 4 onto the opposite corner of the HST unit, right sides together, allowing enough room so that when folded over it will cover the entire corner.

**7.** Stitch the colored snippet, using a scant ¼″ seam.

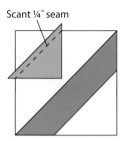

Scant ¼″ seam

- - - - - - - - - - - - - - - - - - - - - - - - - - - - - - - - - - - - - - - - - - - - - - - - - - - - - -

**8.** Press the seam allowance.

**9.** Repeat Steps 3–8 with the other HST unit.

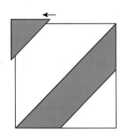

**10.** Trim both striped units to 4½″ × 4½″. The diagonal line of the units must align exactly at the corner of the unit.

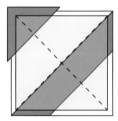 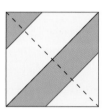

# Constructing the Blocks

**1.** Lay out 2 bow tie end units and 2 striped units as shown.

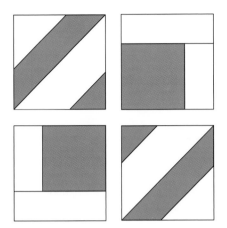

**2.** Sew the units together in rows. Press.

**3.** Sew the rows together to complete the block. Press.

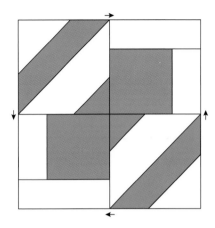

**4.** Repeat Steps 1–3 to make 81 blocks total.

---

# Constructing the Quilt Top

**1.** Lay the blocks out in a 9 × 9 layout, rotating every other block so the striped units create squares on point at the centers of the Bow Tie blocks.

**2.** Sew the blocks together into rows.

**3.** Press the seam allowances in opposite directions in each row.

**4.** Sew the rows together.

**5.** Press the seam allowances in one direction.

---

# Adding the Borders

Follow How to Accurately Apply Borders (page 20) to add the inner and outer borders.

# Finishing

Layer, baste, quilt, and bind as desired.

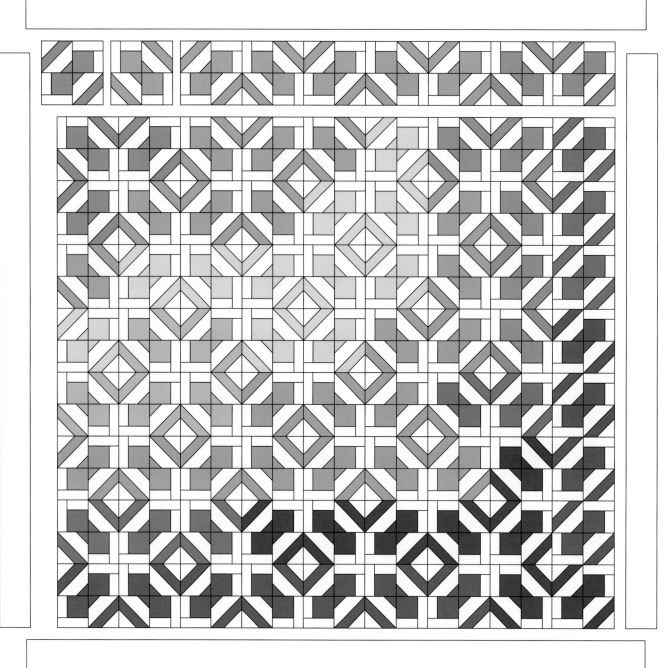

Quilt assembly

# THE CIRCUS COMES TO TOWN

**FINISHED QUILT:** 73½" × 85½"

You may think that this is an odd name for a quilt. Well, it probably is. But when this quilt was finished, I looked at it and it reminded me of one of those large balls that circus elephants balance on. Even though it is made entirely of triangles, it has a look about it that suggests circular motion.

This is an incredibly easy quilt to make. One of its best features is that, like so many of the quilt projects in this book, it can accommodate a wide variety of fabrics.

Most of the colored fabrics in this quilt are medium to dark in value. The "spacing" (page 9) triangles are made from very light fabrics to set them apart. The spacing between the triangles allows the use of diverse fabrics. Don't be afraid to use those large-scale prints.

Creating the triangles involves cutting the 5½" × 5½" squares into trapezoids. Don't be afraid; it's easy!

- - - - - - - - - - - - - - - - - - - - - - - - - - - - - - - - - - - - -

## Materials

- 105 assorted colored scraps, each large enough to yield a 5½" × 5½" square

- 105 assorted light-colored scraps (white, gray, or tonal), each large enough to yield a 5½" × 5½" square

- 1⅛ yards of solid white fabric for borders

- ½ yard of gray fabric for appliqué circles

- 1 yard of woven fusible interfacing, 22" wide

- 82" × 94" backing

- 82" × 94" batting

- ¾ yard for binding

- Teflon or other non-stick pressing sheet (optional)

## Cutting

*See Options for Cutting Scraps (page 8).*

### Colored scraps

- Cut 105 squares 5½" × 5½".

For each pair of 5½" × 5½" squares:

**1.** Place 2 random squares 5½" × 5½" right sides together. Using a fabric marker, mark 1⅛" in from the upper right corner and 1⅛" in from the lower left corner.

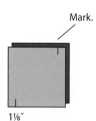

Mark.

1⅛"

**2.** Lay the ruler across the blocks, connecting the 2 marks. Cut.

Cut.

**3.** The top square will yield 2 left trapezoids and the bottom square 2 right trapezoids. Keep the cut pieces in groups of the same shape until all the scraps are cut. Note the 2 right-angle corners at top and bottom. Label them L and R if needed.

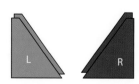

### Light-colored scraps

- Cut 105 squares 5½" × 5½".

Refer to the cutting instructions for colored scraps (at left) to cut all of the 105 light-colored squares into trapezoids.

### White

- Cut 8 strips 4½" × width of fabric for the borders.

### Gray

- Cut 44 circles 3" in diameter for raw-edge appliqué or 3½" for turned-edge appliqué.

### Woven fusible interfacing

- Cut 44 squares 4" × 4".

# Making the Colored Triangles

*All seam allowances are ¼".*

**1.** Mix up each group of L and R colored trapezoids. Pair the pieces so that each pair consists of 1 L and 1 R piece.

**2.** Stitch a pair of trapezoids, right sides together, along the long angled edges. Press the seam allowance open.

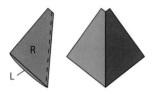

**TIP** *The edge that is sewn is on the bias, so be very careful not to stretch it as you sew and press.*

**3.** Repeat Step 2 to sew a total of 3 colored pairs for 1 block.

**4.** Stitch 2 of the 3 paired units together along the edge of the trapezoid, as shown. Stop exactly at the seam, and backstitch to lock the seam. Press the seam allowance open.

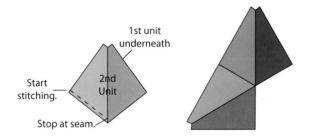

1st unit underneath
2nd Unit
Start stitching.
Stop at seam.

**5.** Sew the third unit to the remaining short edge of the first unit, stopping exactly on the seam and backstitching. Press the seam allowance open. There will be a slight "set-in" seam that occurs when the third piece is added and the triangle is formed.

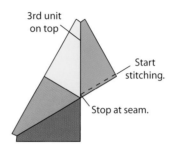

3rd unit on top
Start stitching.
Stop at seam.

**6.** Fold the triangle in half, right sides together. Align the short edges. Sew the last seam as shown to finish the triangle, stopping exactly on the seam and backstitching. Press the seam allowance open.

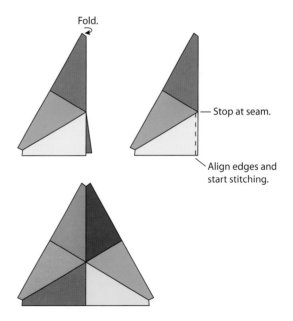

Fold.
Stop at seam.
Align edges and start stitching.

**7.** Repeat Steps 2–6 to make 31 total colored triangles.

# Making the Light Triangles

Make 32 light-colored triangles following Making the Colored Triangles, Steps 1–7 (page 39).

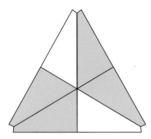

# Making the Side Units

This quilt has half-triangle side units on the end of each row, but they are constructed in a different manner than the full triangles.

Each side unit requires 3 trapezoids. The side units on the left-hand end of a row are mirror images of the side units on the right-hand end of the same row.

Looking at the quilt assembly diagram (next page), you can see that the first/top row has a half-triangle made of 3 trapezoids at the very beginning of the row. It is the right half of a triangle. There is also a partial triangle at the end of the row, made of 3 trapezoids, but it is the left half of the triangle.

## Colored Side Units

### Right-Hand Triangles

**1.** Gather 2 colored right trapezoids and 1 colored left trapezoid.

**2.** Stitch a right trapezoid to a left trapezoid along the long angled edges. Press the seam allowances open.

**3.** Stitch a second right trapezoid to the short side of the left trapezoid, as shown. Press the seam allowances open.

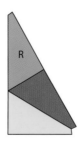

**4.** Repeat Steps 1–3 to make a total of 4 colored right-hand triangles.

### Left-Hand Triangles

**1.** Gather 2 colored left trapezoids and 1 colored right trapezoid.

**2.** Stitch a right trapezoid to a left trapezoid along the long angled edges. Press the seam allowances open.

**3.** Stitch a second *left* trapezoid to the short side of the *right* trapezoid, as shown. Press the seam allowances open.

**4.** Repeat Steps 1–3 to make a total of 4 colored left-hand triangles.

## Light Side Units
### *Left-Hand Triangles*

Repeat Colored Side Units, Left-Hand Triangles, Steps 1–3 (previous page), using 2 light left trapezoids and 1 light right trapezoid. Make a total of 3 light left-hand triangles.

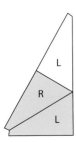

### *Right-Hand Triangles*

Repeat Colored Side Units, Right-Hand Triangles, Steps 1–3 (previous page), using 2 light right trapezoids and 1 light left trapezoid. Make a total of 3 light right-hand triangles.

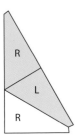

# Putting It All Together

**1.** Refer to the quilt assembly diagram (below) to arrange the full triangles. Fill in the sides with the side triangles. Place the colored triangles point up and the light triangles point down.

**2.** Sew all the triangles together in rows from left to right, backstitching at the beginning and end of each seam. Press the seam allowances open. Handle the quilt top gently to avoid stretching the gaps at the triangle corners.

**3.** Sew all the rows together. Press.

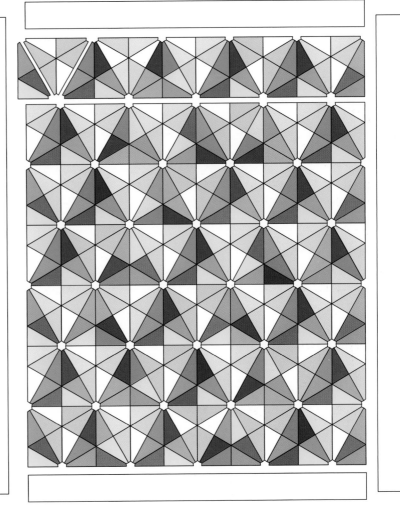

Quilt assembly

# Adding the Borders

Follow How to Accurately Apply Borders (page 20) to add the border.

# Finishing

Layer, baste, quilt, and bind as desired.

# Adding the Circles

**1.** Cover your ironing surface with a Teflon or other nonstick pressing sheet to protect it from fusible residue.

**2.** Place the quilt top *wrong* side up, with the Teflon sheet underneath. Follow the manufacturer's directions to fuse a 4″ × 4″ square of interfacing to the wrong side of the quilt top over each opening, being very careful not to stretch the fabric around each opening.

**3.** On the right side of the quilt top, appliqué the circles over the fused openings using your favorite appliqué technique.

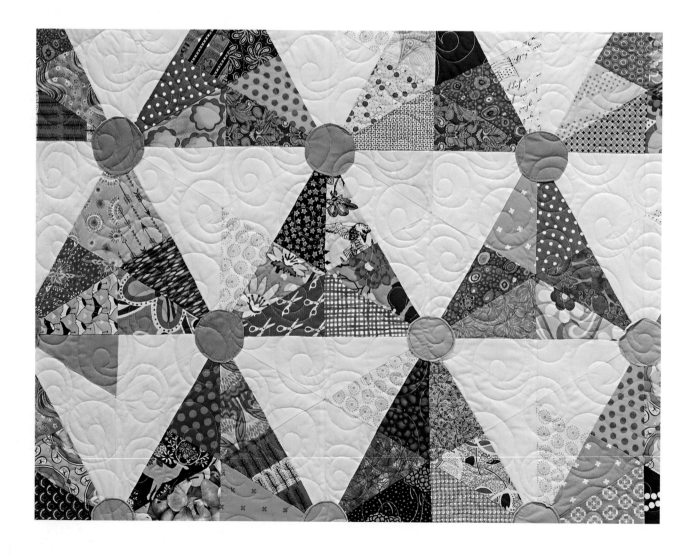

# BLENDED
# HEXAGONS

**FINISHED QUILT:** 63" × 80¼" • **FINISHED BLOCK:** 12½" × 14½" (point to point)

*This quilt is easier than it looks. Each large hexagon ring requires three squares 5½" × 5½" cut from each scrap. When I created this quilt, I was trying to use up my pink and coral scraps.*

*Don't be afraid to use those large-scale prints. Using large-scale prints in monochromatic color schemes helps to create a beautiful blended appearance.*

*This quilt has 32 full hexagon rings, with 6 half-hexagon rings along the right and left sides of the quilt.*

- - - - - - - - - - - - - - - - - - - - - - - - - - - - - - - - - - - - - -

## Materials

- 35 pairs of assorted scraps (70 total), each large enough to yield 3 squares 5½" × 5½"

- 5 assorted solid-color fat quarters of felted wool or cotton for centers

- 1 yard of woven fusible interfacing, 22" wide

- 71" × 88" backing

- 71" × 88" batting

- ⅝ yard for binding

- Regular ruler with 1/16" marks or a rotary cutting ruler with a 60° line

- Teflon or other nonstick pressing sheet (*optional*)

## Cutting

See *Options for Cutting Scraps* (page 8).

### Scraps

- Cut 3 squares 5½" × 5½" from each of the 70 paired fabric scraps (210 squares total).

**TIP** *As soon as you cut the 3 squares from each pair of fabric scraps, re-pair the squares so that you have 1 square of each fabric, right sides together, with the same fabric on top (fabric 1) and the other fabric on the bottom (fabric 2).*

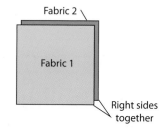

*This is very important. If the order is not maintained, the 2 fabrics in each hexagon won't alternate.*

Subcut the 3 pairs of squares from each set of scraps into trapezoids, using one of the methods below:

**Method 1**: Use this method if you have a ruler marked in sixteenth-inch increments. You will also need a rotary cutting ruler.

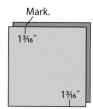

**1.** On each of the 3 pairs of squares, use a marking pencil to mark the top square 1³/16" in from the upper left corner. Make a second mark 1³/16" in from the lower right corner.

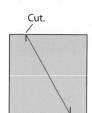

**2.** With a rotary cutting ruler, connect the 2 marks. Cut along the edge of the ruler through both squares of fabric. Repeat this step for all 3 pairs of squares.

**Method 2**: Use this method if you have a rotary cutting ruler with a 60° line.

**1.** On each of the 3 pairs of squares, fold the *top square only* in half vertically and finger-press to crease. Then fold and press it in half horizontally, and crease to mark the exact center.

**2.** Place the creased top squares on top of the bottom squares, right sides together. Align the 60° line on a rotary cutting ruler with the top or bottom of the square, making sure the

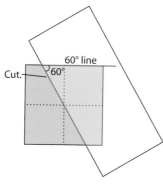

cutting edge runs through the center crease marks, as shown. Cut along the line through both layers. Repeat this step for all 3 pairs of squares.

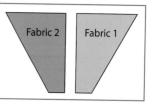

**Note:** *The resulting shapes are trapezoids. Each fabric 1 and fabric 2 pair should consist of mirror-image trapezoids.*

## Solid-color fat quarters

· Cut 38 circles 3″ in diameter.

## Woven fusible interfacing

· Cut 38 squares 4″ × 4″.

# Assembling the Full Hexagons

*All seam allowances are ¼″.*

**1.** Keeping the pairs right sides together, stitch along the straight edge, as shown. Repeat this step with the remaining pairs from 1 set of scraps to make 6 units total. Press the seam allowances open.

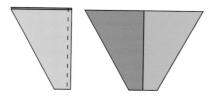

**2.** Place a stitched pair right sides together with another stitched pair, as shown. Stitch them together along the long angled edge.

**3.** Continue to stitch the remaining matching pairs together until you have a hexagon ring.

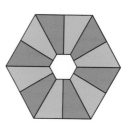

**4.** Press all the seams open.

**5.** Repeat Steps 1–4 to make a total of 32 full hexagon rings.

# Creating the Half-Hexagons

**1.** Follow Assembling the Full Hexagons, Steps 1 and 2 (page 45).

**2.** To make a half-hexagon, add 1 more stitched pair to make a total of 3 pairs of trapezoids.

**3.** Press all the seams open.

**4.** Repeat Steps 1–3 to make a total of 6 half-hexagon rings.

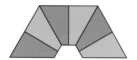

- - - - - - - - - - - - - - - - - - - - - - - - - - - - - - - - - - - - - - - - - - - - - - - - - - - -

# Putting It All Together

Refer to the quilt assembly diagram (page 48) to lay out the hexagons and half-hexagons in 7 rows of 5. Note that the even rows are made of 4 full hexagons and 2 half-hexagons. Sewing all the hexagons together involves some minor Y-seams, but they are not difficult.

## Sewing Row 1

**1.** Align the first and second hexagon in row 1 along the straight vertical edge, right sides together, as shown. Pin as needed to match the seams. Stitch.

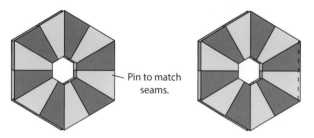

Pin to match seams.

**2.** Press the seam open.

**3.** Repeat Steps 1 and 2 to continue sewing all 5 hexagons in row 1.

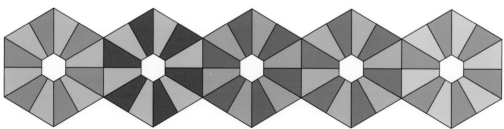

Row 1

# Sewing Row 2

Repeat Sewing Row 1, Steps 1–3 (previous page), but begin and end row 2 with the half-hexagons.

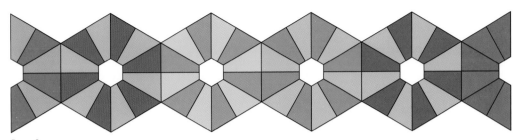

Row 2

# Joining Rows 1 and 2

**Note:** *In the following steps and diagrams, the full hexagons are numbered beginning with the first hexagon in row 1 (1), continuing with hexagon 6 in row 2. The half-hexagons are A (on the left) and B (on the right), as shown.*

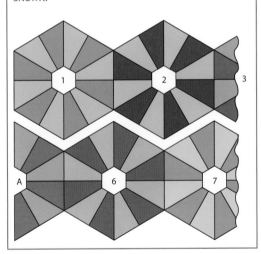

**1.** Pin the left lower edge of hexagon 1 to the top edge of half-hexagon A, right sides together. Match the point and seam allowance of the bottom of hexagon 1 to the seam intersection between half-hexagon A and hexagon 6.

**2.** Stitch, stopping at the seam intersection. Backstitch or lockstitch to lock the seam.

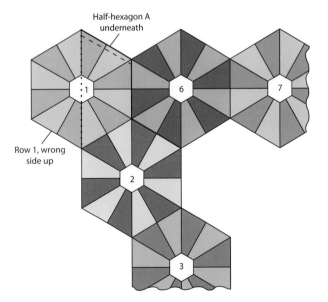

Half-hexagon A underneath

Row 1, wrong side up

**3.** Fold half-hexagon A to align the lower right side of hexagon 1 to the upper left side of hexagon 6, as shown, matching seam intersections. Pin. Stitch hexagon 1 to hexagon 6 from the seam between half-hexagon A and hexagon 6 up to the seam intersection at the point of hexagon 6. Backstitch.

**4.** Repeat Steps 1–3 to align, pin, and stitch all the Row 1 hexagons to Row 2. Make certain to match the seam intersections, to start and stop stitching at the intersections, and to lock the seams. Press.

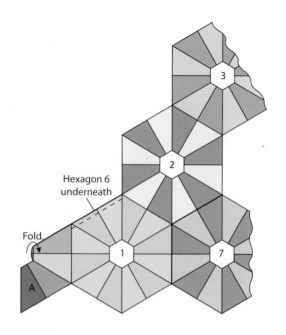

## Sewing the Remaining Rows

**1.** Follow Sewing Row 1 (page 46) and Sewing Row 2 (page 47) to sew all the rows.

**2.** Follow Joining Rows 1 and 2 (page 47) to join each additional row.

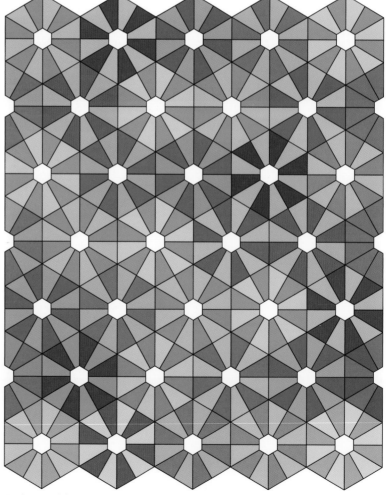

Quilt assembly

# Adding the Circles

**1.** Cover your ironing surface with a Teflon or other nonstick pressing sheet to protect it from fusible residue.

**2.** Place the quilt top *wrong* side up, with the Teflon sheet underneath. Follow the manufacturer's directions to fuse a 4″ × 4″ square of interfacing to the wrong side of the quilt top over each opening, being very careful not to stretch the fabric around each opening.

**3.** On the right side of the quilt top, appliqué the circles over the fused openings using your favorite appliqué technique.

# Finishing

Layer, baste, quilt, and bind as desired.

# ALTERNATIVE BINDING STYLE

Just a few words about the odd angles used for sewing the binding on. They look scarier than they actually are. Don't let them scare you away from this beautiful quilt.

There are many videos online about this very topic. Nevertheless, you just need to remember a couple of simple facts: When you are going around a corner that bumps outward, you will need more fabric to cover the corner, as with a traditional binding that goes around a 90° angle. When you are binding a corner that goes inward, you need less fabric to avoid bunching up.

Going around the angles that bump outward, you can treat them a lot like a 90° angle on a traditional quilt. But here's where it gets a little tricky. Treat your inner angle by straightening it out. Make your sewing edge straight, as shown. Pull the angle open so that your binding and quilt edge are virtually straight. There will be a little hill of quilt to the left, but don't worry about what is not going to be under the needle.

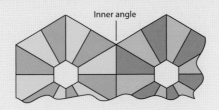
Inner angle

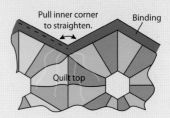
Pull inner corner to straighten. Binding
Quilt top

# STAR BABY

**FINISHED QUILT:** 48½" × 55½"

*The stars on this quilt are positioned in a random fashion, just like the stars in the sky!*

*The holes in the centers are filled with yo-yos, but you could just as easily appliqué circles or any other favorite shape.*

*Some of the stars in this quilt are made from multiple scraps within the same colorway; others are made from matching scraps. Use your creativity. They can be made with whatever fabric placement you like. The instructions are written for stars made of two alternating fabrics.*

## Materials

- 6 pairs of assorted scraps #1 (12 total), each large enough to yield 3 squares 5½" × 5½"

- 1 pair of assorted scraps #2 (2 total), each large enough to yield 3 squares 4½" × 4½"

- 2 pairs of assorted scraps #3 (4 total), each large enough to yield 3 squares 3½" × 3½"

- 2 yards of white for background and outer border

- ½ yard of gray for inner border

- 2 assorted scraps for small yo-yos, each large enough to yield a 4¾"-diameter circle

- 7 assorted scraps for large yo-yos, each large enough to yield a 7"-diameter circle

- 57" × 64" backing

- 57" × 64" batting

- ½ yard for binding

- Regular ruler with ¹⁄₁₆" marks or a rotary cutting ruler with a 60° line

## Cutting

*See Options for Cutting Scraps (page 8).*

### Assorted scraps #1 for 6 large stars

- Cut 3 squares 5½" × 5½" from each of the 12 fabrics.

**TIP** *If you want a star made of 2 alternating fabrics, cut the 3 squares from each pair of fabrics; then re-pair the squares so that you have 1 square of each fabric per pair, right sides together, with the same fabric on top (fabric 1) and the other fabric on the bottom (fabric 2).*

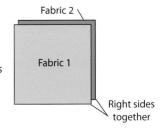

Fabric 2

Fabric 1

Right sides together

### Assorted scraps #2 for 1 medium star

- Cut 3 squares 4½" × 4½" from each of the 2 fabrics.

### Assorted scraps #3 for 2 small stars

- Cut 3 squares 3½" × 3½" from each of the 4 fabrics.

### Cutting the trapezoids

- Subcut the 3 pairs of squares from each set of scraps into trapezoids, using one of the methods below:

**Method 1:** Use this method if you have a ruler marked in sixteenth-inch increments. You will also need a rotary cutting ruler.

**1.** On each of the 3 pairs of squares, use a marking pencil to mark the top square the specified distance in from the upper left corner—1³⁄₁₆" for the large stars, ¹⁵⁄₁₆" for the medium star, and ¾" for the small stars. Make a second mark the same distance in from the lower right corner.

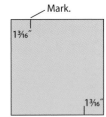

Mark.

1³⁄₁₆"

1³⁄₁₆"

**2.** With a rotary cutting ruler, connect the 2 marks. Cut along the edge of the ruler through both squares of fabric. Repeat this step for all 3 pairs of squares.

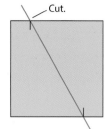

Cut.

**Method 2:** Use this method if you have a rotary cutting ruler with a 60° line.

**1.** On each of the 3 pairs of squares, fold the top square only in half vertically and finger-press to crease. Then fold and press it in half horizontally, and crease to mark the exact center.

**2.** Place the creased top squares on top of the bottom squares, right sides together. Align the 60° line on a rotary cutting ruler with the top or bottom of the square, making sure the

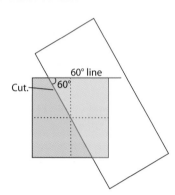

Cut.  60° line  60°

cutting edge runs through the center crease marks, as shown. Cut along the line through both layers. Repeat this step for all 3 pairs of squares.

## White

- Cut 1 rectangle 36½″ × 43½″ for the background.
- Cut 5 strips 4½″ × width of fabric for the outer border.

## Gray

- Cut 5 strips 2½″ × width of fabric for the inner border.

## Scraps for yo-yos

- Cut 2 small circles using the small yo-yo pattern (page 54).
- Cut 7 large circles using the large yo-yo pattern (page 56).

---

# Making the Stars

*All seam allowances are ¼″. Refer to the arrows for pressing direction.*

## Large Stars

**1.** Keep the 2 pairs of trapezoids cut from 2 squares together. Stitch along the long straight edge, right sides together, as shown. Press.

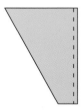

**2.** Stitch along the upper short edge, as shown.

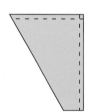

**3.** Turn right side out. Push the point out with a bodkin, chopstick, or knitting needle.

**4.** Fold the top of the unit down, aligning the top seam with the center seam, as shown. Press the seam allowance to one side by inserting your iron up and into the point, and then pressing the seam allowance inside the point the same direction. Press the trapezoid unit flat.

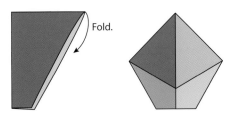

**5.** Repeat Steps 1–4 to stitch and press all 6 sets of trapezoid pairs.

**6.** Stitch 3 trapezoid units together, as shown.

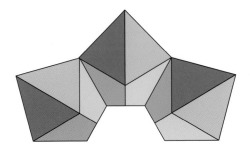

**7.** Continue stitching trapezoid units together to make a hexagon ring with a small center opening. Press the seam allowances open.

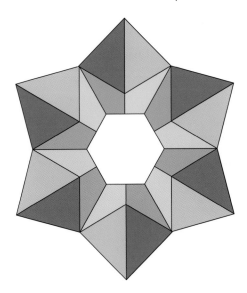

**8.** Repeat Steps 1–7 to make a total of 6 large stars.

## Medium Star

Follow Large Stars, Steps 1–7 (previous page), using the 4½″ × 4½″ squares to make 1 medium star.

## Small Stars

Follow Large Stars, Steps 1–7 (previous page), using the 3½″ × 3½″ squares to make 2 small stars.

- - - - - - - - - - - - - - - - - - - - - - - - - - - - - - - - -

# Putting It All Together

## Adding the Borders

Follow How to Accurately Apply Borders (page 20) to add the inner and outer borders to the 36½″ × 43½″ background rectangle.

## Appliquéing the Stars

**1.** Randomly position the stars on the quilt top and pin in place.

**2.** Using your favorite appliqué technique, appliqué the stars to the background.

## Making the Yo-Yos

The open centers of the stars are covered by yo-yos. Use the small yo-yo pattern for the small stars and the large yo-yo pattern for the medium and large stars.

**1.** Fold and press under ¼" around the circle, wrong sides together.

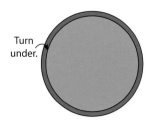

Turn under.

**2.** Hand sew a running stitch through the folded edge around the circle.

Running stitch.

**3.** When the stitching meets the beginning of the stitching, pull the thread so the entire circumference gathers onto itself, closing off the wrong side of the fabric. Take a stitch into the fabric again and make a hidden knot.

**4.** Flatten the yo-yo.

**5.** Appliqué the yo-yos into the centers of the stars.

# Finishing

Layer, baste, quilt, and bind as desired.

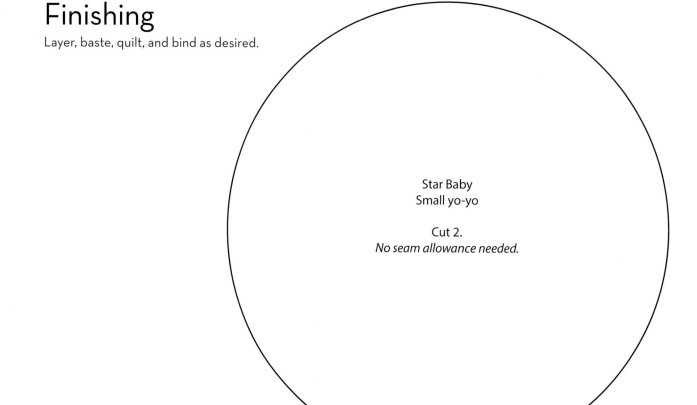

Star Baby
Small yo-yo

Cut 2.
*No seam allowance needed.*

Quilt assembly

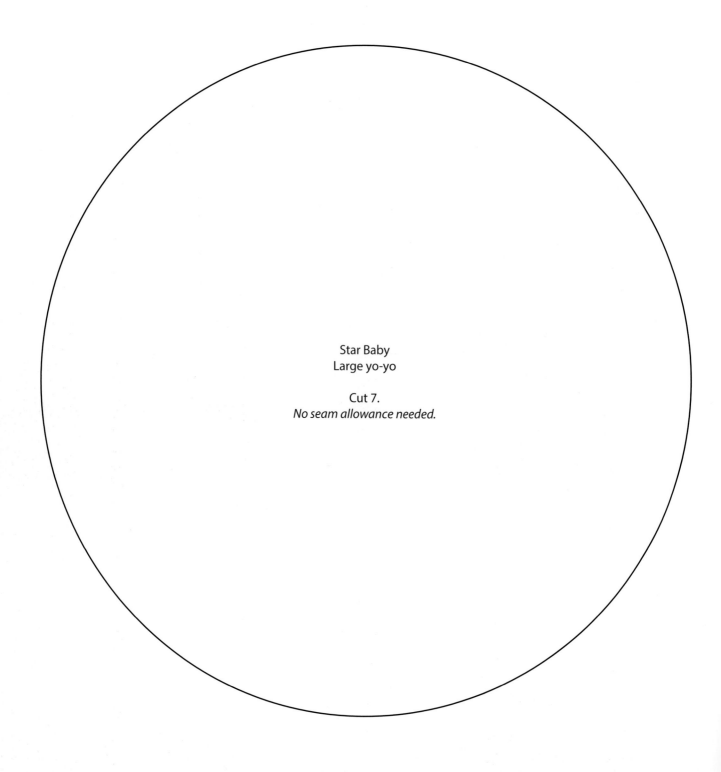

Star Baby
Large yo-yo

Cut 7.
*No seam allowance needed.*

**FINISHED QUILT:** 57½" × 70½" • **FINISHED BLOCKS:** A: 10" × 6", B: 10" × 3"

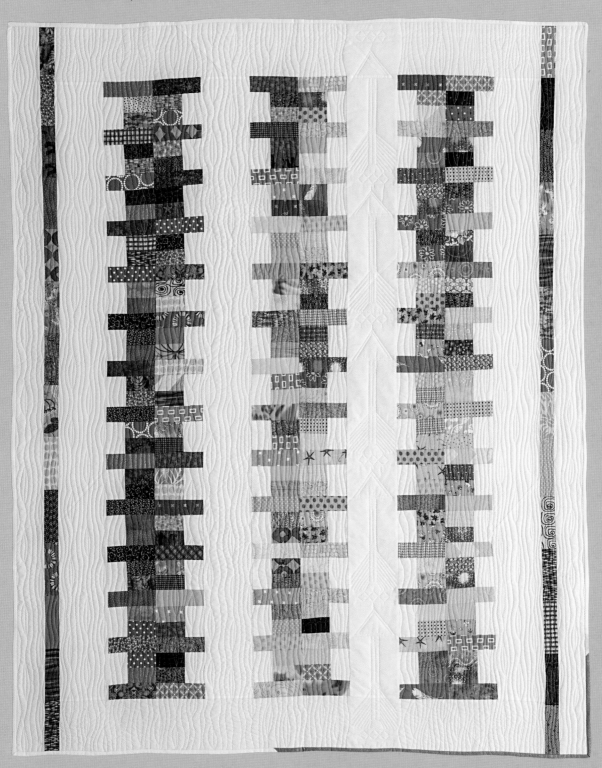

*This quilt will use up some of the smaller scraps in your stash. If you have leftovers from making Packages, Boxes, and Bows, you could put them to work here, but this quilt certainly stands on its own!*

---

## Materials

- 112 assorted scraps, each large enough to yield a 2″ × 5½″ rectangle
- 156 assorted scraps, each large enough to yield a 2″ × 3½″ rectangle
- 2¾ yards of white for background and borders
- 66″ × 79″ backing
- 66″ × 79″ batting
- ⅝ yard for binding

## Cutting

*See Options for Cutting Scraps (page 8).*

### Scraps

- Cut 112 rectangles 2″ × 5½″ (A); set aside 28 for the inner borders.
- Cut 156 rectangles 2″ × 3½″ (B).

### White

- Cut 5 strips 3½″ × width of fabric; subcut 78 rectangles 2½″ × 3½″ (C).
- Cut 8 strips 5″ × width of fabric for the sashing.
- Cut 3 strips 5½″ × width of fabric for the top and bottom borders.
- Cut 4 strips 3½″ × width of fabric for the outer side border.

> **Note:** Label the rectangles if needed.
>
> [A] Colored 2″ × 5½″ A rectangle
>
> [B] Colored 2″ × 3½″ B rectangle
>
> [C] White 2½″ × 3½″ C rectangle

> **Important:** It is very important that you use an accurate ¼″ seam allowance when stitching the blocks together, or your sashing will not fit and your quilt will not lay flat. To be sure, refer to ¼″ Seam Allowances (page 18) to set and test your seam allowances.

# Making the Blocks

*All seam allowances are ¼". Follow the arrows for pressing directions.*

Blocks A and B both begin with the same inner section, Unit 1, sewn from B and C pieces. Block A adds outer A rectangles. Work in monochromatic groupings as much as possible for a color arrangement like that of the finished quilt.

## Unit 1's

**1.** Place 2 B rectangles right sides together and stitch along the long edge. Press.

**2.** Add a solid C rectangle, as shown, and stitch. Press.

**3.** Repeat Steps 1 and 2 to make a total of 78 Unit 1's; set aside 36 for the B blocks.

---

## A Blocks

**1.** Add an A rectangle in the same color family to a Unit 1, as shown, and stitch. Press.

**2.** Add a second A rectangle to the opposite side of the unit and stitch. Press.

**3.** Repeat Steps 1 and 2 to add A rectangles to a total of 42 Unit 1's.

**4.** To complete each A block, sew 2 units from Step 3 together as shown, nesting the seam allowances. Press.

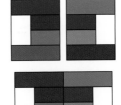

**5.** Repeat Step 4 to make a total of 21 A blocks.

---

## B Blocks

**1.** Sew 2 Unit 1's together as shown, nesting the seam allowances. Press.

**2.** Repeat Step 1 to make a total of 18 B blocks.

# Assembling the Quilt

## Creating the Columns

**1.** Each column is made of 7 A blocks and 6 B blocks. Refer to the quilt assembly diagram (next page) to lay out the blocks in rainbow order or as desired.

**2.** Sew an A block to the top and bottom of a B block, as shown. Press.

**3.** Repeat Step 2 to sew 3 columns.

## Making the Inner Sashing Strips

**TIP** *Each column should measure 60½". If your columns are different lengths, you will need to rip out some block seams, adjust your seam allowance, and re-stitch. Measure the columns and cut the sashing to fit.*

**1.** Trim the selvages from the 5" × width of fabric sashing strips. Join in pairs.

**2.** Press the seam allowance to one side.

**3.** Trim each sashing strip to 60½", staggering where you have the joining seam, so the seams will not fall in the same place when joining them to the columns.

## Sewing the Sashing to the Columns

**1.** Pin and then sew the sashing strips between the columns, right sides together.

**TIP** *If either the sashing strip or the column is slightly longer, you will need to ease it to fit. See Fitting Tips for Columns (page 62).*

**2.** Press the seam allowances toward the columns.

## Adding the Top and Bottom Border

**1.** Trim the selvages from the 5½" × width of fabric strips. Sew them together end to end into 1 continuous strip. Press the seam allowances to one side.

**2.** Follow How to Accurately Apply Borders (page 20) to add the top and bottom borders.

## Making the Scrappy Inner Border

**1.** Join 14 A rectangles, short end to short end, right sides together, and stitch. Press as desired.

**2.** Repeat Step 1 to make a second scrappy border.

# Adding the Inner and Outer Borders

Follow How to Accurately Apply Borders (page 20) to add the inner and outer borders. Press toward the scrappy border.

# Finishing

Layer, baste, quilt, and bind as desired.

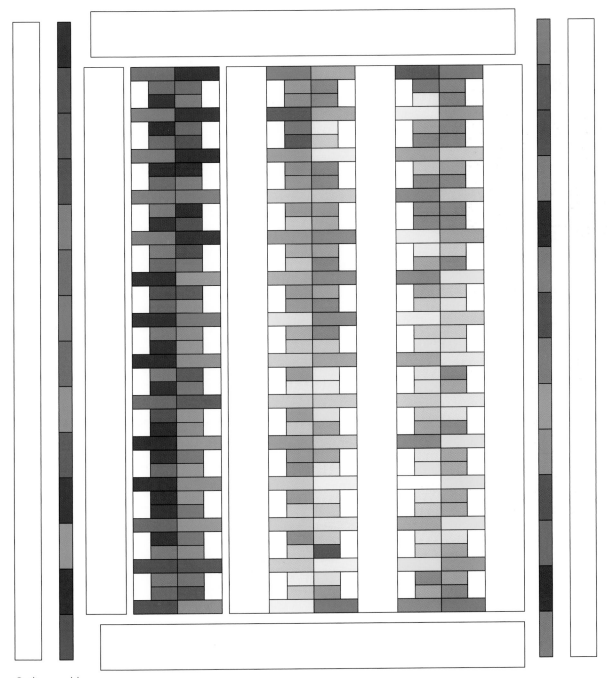

Quilt assembly

# FITTING TIPS FOR COLUMNS

If the ¼" seam allowance isn't always accurate, or if there are other piecing errors, it may be difficult to make a pieced unit or column fit together with other pieced columns and sashing strips.

If all your pieced columns (or rows) are all the same size but don't match the cut sizes listed, simply cut sashing and borders to fit what you have.

If your columns or rows are different sizes, look over your pieced units carefully to make sure you have sewn all the blocks correctly. Look to see if any of your seam allowances appear incorrect. If you see an obvious problem, fix it.

Small discrepancies in length can be eased in when sewing long seams.

**1.** Fold your column in half to find the center of the column, and pin or mark it.

**2.** Find and mark the center of your sashing in the same manner.

**3.** Pin the column and sashing together at the centers.

> **Note:** *Pin so that the longer of the two will be on the bottom, next to the feed dogs.*

**4.** Pin the ends together.

**5.** Continue pinning between the end pins and the center pin, evenly dividing any excess.

**6.** Sew the 2 pieces together, placing the section that is a bit longer next to the feed dogs. The piece that is a bit shorter will be on the top, next to the presser foot. The feed dogs will help to push through any extra fabric. Press.

> **Note:** *Of course, if you have two sections of quilt that you are trying to pin together and they are grossly mismatched, you are going to have to spend a little more quality time with your seam ripper.*

A common mistake among beginners is to believe that all is well even if there is a small discrepancy in length. The beginner may stretch one piece or another a little to make it work and then add the next column. But if the first ones were not right, they cannot be made right by adding additional pieces. The entire piece will be too distorted when it is finished, and salvaging it will not be possible.

It is always best to find the correct measurement by multiplying the size of your blocks or units by the number of units in the column or row. Always make your sashing to fit the number it should be, not the number it actually is.

This information should be of benefit with all quilting projects.

# OWL'S WELL THAT ENDS WELL

**FINISHED QUILT:** 60½" × 60½" • **FINISHED BLOCK:** 20" × 20"

*Whooo can resist a friendly owl?*

*I am frequently the recipient of homeless fabric. While most of us don't think fabric could ever be homeless, believe me, it can.*

*One of my customers and good friends challenged me. She was cleaning out the "brown" section of her sewing room. She brought me an entire bag of browns and said, "Let's see what you do with these." So here's what I did.*

**TIP** *The beaks and the feet of the owls are supposed to be slightly wonky, since you are using odd yellow snippets and scraps.*

- - - - - - - - - - - - - - - - - - - - - - - - - - - - - - - - - - - -

## Materials

- Assorted scraps in 9 different colorways, each colorway group large enough to yield 4 squares 3½″ × 3½″ and 6 squares 5½″ × 5½″
- 9 assorted dark brown scraps, each large enough to yield 2 squares 5½″ × 5½″
- 9 assorted medium brown scraps, each large enough to yield 4 squares 5½″ × 5½″
- 9 assorted light brown scraps, each large enough to yield 2 squares 5½″ × 5½″
- Assorted gold or yellow snippets and scraps for beaks and feet
- 2½ yards of white fabric for background
- 69″ × 69″ backing
- 69″ × 69″ batting
- ⅝ yard for binding

## Cutting

*See Options for Cutting Scraps (page 8).*

For each Owl block (9 total):

### SCRAPS (FROM 1 COLORWAY)

- Cut 4 squares 3½″ × 3½″.
- Cut 6 squares 5½″ × 5½″.

### DARK BROWN SCRAPS

- Cut 2 squares 5½″ × 5½″.

### MEDIUM BROWN SCRAPS

- Cut 4 squares 5½″ × 5½″.

### LIGHT BROWN SCRAPS

- Cut 2 squares 5½″ × 5½″.

### WHITE

- Cut 12 squares 5½″ × 5½″.

# Making the Owl Blocks

*All seam allowances are ¼". Refer to the arrows for pressing directions.*

Use method 2 for making half-square triangles (page 19).

## Making Row 1 of the Owl Block

**1.** Lay a colored 3½" × 3½" square on the lower right corner of a white square, right sides together, as shown.

**2.** Using a water-soluble marking pencil, draw a diagonal line from corner to corner on the colored square. Stitch directly on the line.

**3.** Fold back the corner of the white square away from the stitching line. Trim off the corner of the colored square ¼" from the stitching line, as shown, leaving the corner of the white square intact.

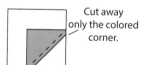

Cut away only the colored corner.

**TIP** *Keeping the white square intact, rather than trimming it off with the colored square, will help you to keep the unit a true 5½" × 5½" throughout the sewing process. When joining the units, you will know exactly where the true ¼" seam allowance should be.*

**4.** Fold the remaining colored square over to the outside corner and press.

**5.** Repeat Steps 1–4 to make a mirror-image unit. These are the ear tuft units.

**6.** Stitch the 2 owl-ear units and 2 white squares into a row, as shown. Press.

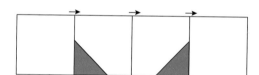

## Making Row 2 of the Owl Block

**1.** Using 2 light brown squares and 2 dark brown squares, make 2 half-square triangle (HST) units using method 2 (page 19). Press the seam allowance toward the darker fabric.

**2.** Lay a colored 3½″ × 3½″ square over the dark brown corner of a HST unit, right sides together.

**3.** Using a water-soluble marking pencil, draw a diagonal line from corner to corner on the 3½″ × 3½″square. Stitch directly on the line.

**4.** Fold back the corner of the dark brown triangle. Trim off the corner of the colored square ¼″ from the stitching line, as shown, leaving the corner of the original HST unit intact.

**5.** Fold the remaining colored triangle over to the outside corner and press.

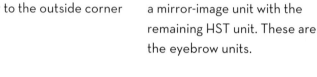

**6.** Repeat Steps 2–5 to make a mirror-image unit with the remaining HST unit. These are the eyebrow units.

Stitch.

—Trim.

**7.** Stitch the 2 eyebrow units and 2 white squares together into a row, as shown. Press.

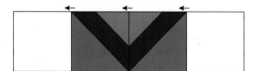

- - - - - - - - - - - - - - - - - - - - - - - - - - - - - - - - - - - - - - - - - - -

## Making Row 3 of the Owl Block

**1.** Using 2 white squares and 2 colored squares 5½″ × 5½″, make 2 HST units for the upper wing units. Press the seam allowance toward the darker fabric.

**2.** Using 2 medium brown squares and 2 colored squares 5½″ × 5½″, make 2 HST units for the upper body units. Press the seam allowance toward the darker fabric.

**3.** Randomly cut 2 triangles 1½″–2″ from yellow or gold scraps.

**4.** Lay a triangle over the upper right corner of an upper body HST unit, right sides together. Make sure that the triangle will be large enough to cover the corner of the unit when stitched and flipped. Stitch across the long edge of the triangle.

**5.** Fold the triangle over to the corner of the HST unit, and press.

**6.** Flip the unit wrong side up and trim the yellow triangle even with the edges of the unit.

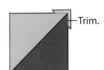

Trim.

**7.** Repeat Steps 4–6 to make a mirror-image upper body unit.

**8.** Stitch the upper wing and upper body units together into a row, as shown. Press.

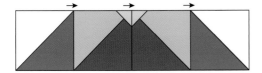

## Making Row 4 of the Owl Block

**1.** Using 2 colored squares 5½″ × 5½″ and 2 white squares, make 2 HST units for the lower wing units. Press toward the colored fabric.

**2.** Using 2 white squares and 2 medium brown squares, make 2 HST units. Press toward the brown fabric. These are the body/foot units.

**3.** Randomly cut 2 triangles from yellow or gold scraps.

**4.** Lay a triangle over the bottom right corner of a body/foot unit, right sides together. Make sure that the triangle will be large enough to cover the corner of the unit when stitched and flipped. Stitch across the long edge of the triangle.

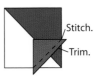

Stitch.

Trim.

**5.** Fold the triangle over to the corner of the HST unit and press.

**6.** Flip the unit wrong side up and trim the yellow triangle even with the edges of the unit.

Trim.

**7.** Repeat Steps 3–6 to make a mirror-image body/foot unit.

**8.** Stitch the lower wing and body/foot units together into a row, as shown. Press.

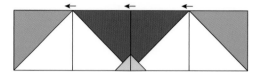

---

## Completing the Owl Blocks

*In order to press seam allowances so they will nest easily from block to block, you will need to decide on the layout of the blocks before assembling each block.*

**1.** Follow the instructions for making rows 1, 2, 3, and 4 of the Owl block (pages 65–68) to make all the units and rows for a total of 9 blocks. Do *not* sew the block rows together into blocks yet.

**2.** Lay out the 4 rows for each block, as shown in the block assembly diagram (at right) and quilt assembly diagram (next page).

**3.** Join the block rows together into blocks.

**4.** Press the row seam allowances in each block in alternating directions.

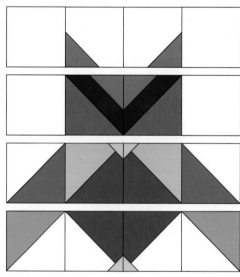

Block assembly

# Putting It All Together

1. Sew the blocks into rows.

2. Press the seam allowances in each row in alternating directions.

3. Sew the rows together.

4. Press all the seam allowances in one direction.

# Finishing

Layer, baste, quilt, and bind as desired.

Quilt assembly

# WILLIAM TELL

**FINISHED QUILT:** 72½" × 72½" · **FINISHED BLOCK:** 24" × 24"

**FINISHED ARROWS:** Large: 8" × 24", Small: 6" × 24", Border: 6" × varied lengths

Arrows are appealing. What makes them so appealing, I think, is that they are symbolic in a number of ways.

Cupid comes along and shoots his arrow into someone's heart and he or she falls in love. Many think of arrows as a symbol of our nation's Native American heritage. Others may think of William Tell, the legendary marksman with a crossbow.

I like them because they have colorful feathers. Who doesn't like colorful feathers?

This quilt employs a lot of negative space, so the sky's the limit for your creativity. You can use large-scale prints and prints you didn't think you'd use again. There's a monochromatic theme within each arrow. That eliminates a ton of anxiety when choosing fabrics. If one arrow is blue, just pick out a bunch of different blues. They're sure to go together!

> **Note**
> - This quilt is made up of 4 large 24″ × 24″ blocks: 2 blocks have 2 large arrows and 2 blocks have 2 small and 1 large arrow.
> - The border is made up of small arrows.
> - Arrow shafts are appliquéd using your preferred method after the arrow units are pieced.
> - Block and border materials and cutting are listed separately.

## Materials

For large arrows:

- 3 assorted red scraps, each large enough to yield 4 squares 4½″ × 4½″

- 3 assorted pink scraps, each large enough to yield 4 squares 4½″ × 4½″

- 3 assorted orange scraps, each large enough to yield 4 squares 4½″ × 4½″

- 3 assorted yellow scraps, each large enough to yield 4 squares 4½″ × 4½″

- 3 assorted green scraps, each large enough to yield 4 squares 4½″ × 4½″

- 3 assorted blue scraps, each large enough to yield 4 squares 4½″ × 4½″

For small arrows:

- 3 assorted red scraps, each large enough to yield 4 squares 3½″ × 3½″

- 6 assorted green scraps, each large enough to yield 4 squares 3½″ × 3½″

- 3 assorted blue scraps, each large enough to yield 4 squares 3½″ × 3½″

For arrowheads:

- Assorted gray scraps, enough to yield 12 squares 4½″ × 4½″ and 8 squares 3½″ × 3½″

For arrow shafts:

- Assorted brown scraps, not more than 12 strips 1″ × 13″ (amount will vary based on preferred appliqué method)

Other materials

- 3⅛ yards of white for block backgrounds, sashing, and inner border

- 81″ × 81″ backing

- 81″ × 81″ batting

- ⅝ yard for binding

> **Note:** See Making the Borders (page 75) for materials and cutting for the borders.

## Cutting

*See Options for Cutting Scraps (page 8).*

### Colored scraps

**LARGE ARROWS**

- From each colorway grouping of 3 scraps, cut the following:

  4 squares 4½" × 4½" per scrap (12 total per colorway; 72 total)

**SMALL ARROWS**

- From each colorway grouping of 3 scraps, cut the following:

  4 squares 3½" × 3½" per scrap (12 total per colorway; 48 total)

### White

- Cut 19 strips 4½" × width of fabric.

  *Subcut the following:*

  8 rectangles 4½" × 24" for the sashing

  48 squares 4½" × 4½" for the large arrows

  Set the remaining 8 strips aside for the row sashing and inner border.

**SMALL ARROWS**

- Cut 5 strips 3½" × width of fabric.

  Subcut 48 squares 3½" × 3½".

### Gray scraps

**LARGE ARROWS**

- Cut 6 pairs of matching squares 4½" × 4½" (12 total).

**SMALL ARROWS**

- Cut 4 pairs of matching squares 3½" × 3½" (8 total).

- - - - - - - - - - - - - - - - - - - - - - - - - - - - - - - - - - - - -

# Making the Arrow Blocks

*All seam allowances are ¼". Press toward the darker fabric when making the half-square triangle (HST) units. Follow the arrows for pressing direction.*

Use method 2 (page 19) to make the HST units.

## Large Arrow Units

The large arrow units are made of an arrowhead, a shaft, and 3 feathers. The shaft is appliquéd after the blocks are constructed.

To make 1 large arrow unit, you will need:

8 white squares 4½" × 4½"

2 matching gray squares 4½" × 4½"

3 sets of 4 matching squares 4½" × 4½" in the same colorway (A, B, C)

Label the matching squares if needed, or make a key for yourself.

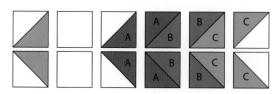

**1.** For the arrowhead, sew 2 matching white/gray HST units.

**2.** For the feathers, sew the following HST units:

2 matching
white/A

2 matching
B/C

2 matching
A/B

2 matching
C/white

**3.** Sew all the matching HST units together into pairs, rotating 1 HST unit in each pair as shown. Press.

**4.** Sew 2 white 4½″ × 4½″ squares together. Press.

**5.** Lay out the paired arrowhead, white, and feather units as shown. Sew together to make a large arrow unit. Press all seams toward the arrowhead.

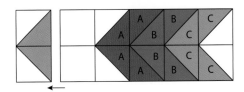

**6.** Repeat Steps 1–5 to make a total of 6 large arrow units.

## Small Arrow Units

The small arrow units are made of an arrowhead, a longer shaft, and 3 feathers. The shaft is appliquéd after the blocks are constructed.

To make 1 small arrow unit, you will need:

  12 white squares 3½" × 3½"

  2 matching gray squares 3½" × 3½"

  3 sets of 4 matching squares 3½" × 3½" in the same colorway (A, B, C)

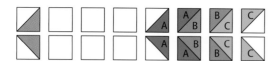

1. Repeat Large Arrow Units, Steps 1–3 (page 72), using the 3½" × 3½" squares.

2. Sew 2 white 3½" × 3½" squares together. Repeat this step to make a total of 3 white pairs. Press the seams in one direction.

3. Lay out the paired arrowhead, white, and feather units as shown. Rotate the white pairs as needed so the seams nest. Sew together to make a small arrow unit. Press all seams away from the arrowhead.

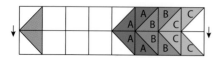

4. Repeat Steps 1–3 to make a total of 4 small arrow units.

## Three-Arrow Blocks

1. Arrange 2 small arrow units and 1 large arrow unit with a 4½" × 24½" block sashing strip, as shown in the block assembly diagrams.

2. Sew the units together. Press.

3. Repeat Steps 1 and 2 to make a second three-arrow block, as shown.

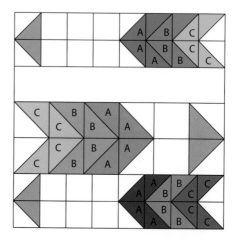

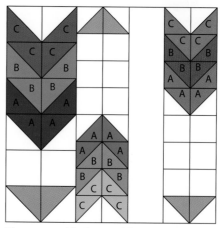

Three-arrow block assembly

## Two-Arrow Blocks

**1.** Arrange 2 large arrow units with 2 block sashing strips 4½" × 24½", as shown in the block assembly diagram.

**2.** Sew the units together. Press.

**3.** Repeat Steps 1 and 2 to make a second two-arrow block, as shown.

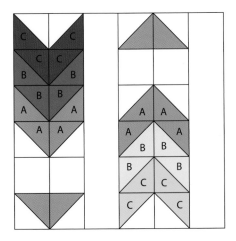

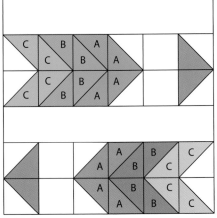

Two-arrow block assembly

# Making the Borders

*All seam allowances are ¼". Press toward the darker fabric when making HST units. Follow the arrows for pressing direction.*

The outer border is sewn entirely from 3½" × 3½" squares, but the lengths of the shaft sections vary. Shafts will be appliquéd after the borders are constructed.

Use method 2 (page 19) to make the HST units.

## Materials

For border arrows:

- 3 assorted pink scraps, each large enough to yield 4 squares 3½" × 3½"

- 3 assorted red scraps #1, each large enough to yield 4 squares 3½" × 3½"

- 3 assorted red scraps #2, each large enough to yield 4 squares 3½" × 3½"

- 4 assorted yellow scraps, each large enough to yield 4 squares 3½" × 3½"

- 3 assorted green scraps, each large enough to yield 4 squares 3½" × 3½"

- 3 assorted blue scraps #1, each large enough to yield 4 squares 3½" × 3½"

- 3 assorted blue scraps #2, each large enough to yield 4 squares 3½" × 3½"

- 3 assorted purple scraps #1, each large enough to yield 4 squares 3½" × 3½"

- 4 assorted purple scraps #2, each large enough to yield 4 squares 3½" × 3½"

- 4 assorted brown scraps, each large enough to yield 4 squares 3½" × 3½"

Other materials

- Assorted gray scraps, enough to yield 20 squares 3½" × 3½" for arrowheads

- 1⅜ yards white for background

## Cutting

*See Options for Cutting Scraps (page 8).*

Colored scraps

From each colorway grouping of 3 or 4 scraps, cut the following:

• 4 squares 3½″ × 3½″ per scrap (12 or 16 per colorway; 132 total)

Gray scraps

• Cut 10 pairs of matching squares 3½″ × 3½″ (20 total).

White

• Cut 12 strips 3½″ × width of fabric. Subcut 130 squares 3½″ × 3½″.

# Top Border

**1.** Follow Small Arrow Units (page 74) to make a red border arrow unit and a green border arrow unit, but only use 2 pairs of white 3½″ × 3½″ squares, as shown.

**2.** Sew 3 four-patches of white 3½″ × 3½″ squares. Press seams in alternate directions so they nest.

**3.** Sew the 2 border arrows and 3 four-patches together as shown to make the top border. Rotate the four-patches as needed so the seams will nest.

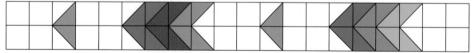

Top border

# Bottom Border

**1.** Follow Small Arrow Units (page 74) to make a pink border arrow, but only use 2 pairs of white 3½″ × 3½″ squares, as shown.

**2.** Follow Small Arrow Units (page 74) to make a brown border arrow, but make an additional colored HST unit and 4 pairs of white 3½″ × 3½″ squares, as shown.

3. Sew 2 white 3½″ × 3½″ squares together to make a two-patch. Press.

4. Sew 1 four-patch of white 3½″ × 3½″ squares. Press seams in alternate directions so they nest.

5. Sew the 2 border arrows and white two- and four-patches together as shown to make the bottom border. Rotate the white units as needed so the seams will nest.

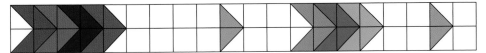

Bottom border

## Left Border

1. Follow Small Arrow Units (page 74) to make a red border arrow.

2. Follow Small Arrow Units (page 74) to make a blue border arrow, but only use 1 pair of white 3½″ × 3½″ squares, as shown.

3. Follow Small Arrow Units (page 74) to make a purple border arrow, but make an additional colored HST unit and only use 2 pairs of white 3½″ × 3½″ squares, as shown.

4. Sew 2 white 3½″ × 3½″ squares together to make a two-patch. Press.

5. Sew a four-patch of white 3½″ × 3½″ squares. Press seams in alternate directions so they nest.

6. Sew the 2 border arrows and white two- and four-patches together as shown to make the left side border. Rotate the white units as needed so the seams will nest.

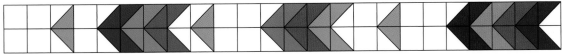

Left side border

## Right Border

**1.** Follow Small Arrow Units (page 74) to make a blue border arrow and a purple border arrow, but only use 1 pair of white 3½″ × 3½″ squares, as shown.

**2.** Follow Small Arrow Units (page 74) to make a yellow border arrow, but make an additional colored HST unit and only use 2 pairs of white 3½″ × 3½″ squares, as shown.

**3.** Sew 2 white 3½″ × 3½″ squares together to make a two-patch. Repeat to make a second two-patch. Press.

**4.** Sew a four-patch of white 3½″ × 3½″ squares. Press seams in alternate directions so they nest.

**5.** Sew the 2 border arrows and white two- and four-patches together as shown to make the right side border. Rotate the white units as needed so the seams will nest.

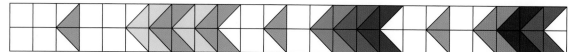

Right side border

# Putting It All Together

**1.** Refer to the quilt assembly diagram (next page) to sew the arrow blocks together in 2 rows of 2 with a 4½″ × 24½″ sashing strip between them.

**2.** Sew the 8 remaining 4½″ × width of fabric strips together end to end for the horizontal sashing and inner border. Press.

**3.** Cut a strip 4½″ × 52½″ for the horizontal sashing. Sew the 2 rows together with the sashing.

**4.** Refer to How to Accurately Apply Borders (page 20) to measure, cut, and attach the inner border. The side borders should measure 52½″ long and the top and bottom should be 60½″. The inner border is sewn to the sides first and then the top and bottom. Press toward the center.

**5.** Sew the top and bottom arrow borders to the quilt. Press. Sew the left and right side arrow borders to the quilt. Press toward the center.

# Adding the Arrow Shafts

**1.** Cut brown strips (with or without seam allowances, depending on your chosen appliqué method), so the finished width after appliquéing is approximately ½".

**2.** Appliqué the brown strips to the quilt top between the arrowheads and the feather section of the arrows, using your preferred method.

# Finishing

Layer, baste, quilt, and bind as desired.

Quilt assembly

# CLINGING VINE

**FINISHED QUILT:** 57½" × 60½"

*Making this quilt will have you plowing through your scraps. It is made in a monochromatic fashion. It really alleviates "patch-match anxiety disorder"! The fabrics are going to work together because the colors are strategically located within their color family.*

*The biggest decision that you will have to make is which colors to use for your columns.*

*This quilt is perfect for using up the odd-shaped scraps in your stash. You only need enough of each scrap to allow you to cut a 5½" × 5½" square.*

- - - - - - - - - - - - - - - - - - - - - - - - - - - - - - - - - - - - - - - - - - -

## Materials

*For the quilt as shown, refer to Cutting (at right) for the specific quantities to cut from each color.*

- 90 assorted colored scraps, each large enough to yield a square 5½" × 5½"

- 90 assorted white and cream tonal scraps, each large enough to yield a square 5½" × 5½"

- ¾ yard total of white and off-white tonal prints for sashing

- 66" × 69" backing

- 66" × 69" batting

- ⅝ yard for binding

## Cutting

*See Options for Cutting Scraps (page 8).*

### Colored scraps

- Cut 90 squares 5½" × 5½", or cut the following quantities of squares 5½" × 5½" from each color:

  Orange: 30

  Aqua: 26

  Green: 26

  Red: 4

  Pink: 4

### White and cream tonal scraps

- Cut 90 squares 5½" × 5½".

### White and off-white tonal prints

- Cut 4 strips 5" × width of fabric.

# Constructing the Blocks

*All seam allowances are ¼". Follow the arrows for pressing direction.*

## Making the Half-Square Triangle Units

**1.** Make 90 color/white half-square triangle (HST) units, using method 1 (page 18). Keep the matching HST units together in pairs.

**2.** Trim each HST unit to 4½" × 4½", making sure that the seamline runs exactly from corner to corner.

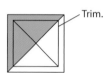

Trim.

- - - - - - - - - - - - - - - - - - - - - - - - - - - - - -

# Assembling the Quilt

*The quilt is assembled in columns rather than in rows. See Fitting Tips for Columns (page 62).*

Refer to the quilt assembly diagram (next page) to lay out 3 columns of 4 HST units (2 matching pairs) per row. Rotate the HST units as needed to match the orientation shown. Note that the placement of the units in the bottom row is reversed.

## Making the Columns

*Work 1 row at a time within each column to avoid confusion and allow for pressing seams to nest.*

**1.** Sew the matching HST units in the first row of Column 1 together in 2 pairs along the colored sides, as shown. Press both seams to the right.

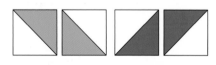

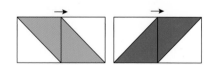

**2.** Sew the paired HST units together along the white sides, as shown. Press the seam to the right.

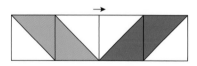

**3.** Repeat Steps 1 and 2 to sew the remaining rows in each column together, alternating the pressing direction in each row. Pin as needed to match the seam intersections. Remember that the last row in each column is a mirror image of the previous row.

## Making and Adding the Sashing

**1.** Follow the instructions for Color Brick Road, Making the Inner Sashing Strips (page 60) and Sewing the Sashing to the Columns (page 60) to add the 5″ sashing strips between the columns. I chose to use diagonal seams when joining the sashing to mimic the HST seams.

**2.** Press the seam allowances toward the sashing.

# Finishing

Layer, baste, quilt, and bind as desired.

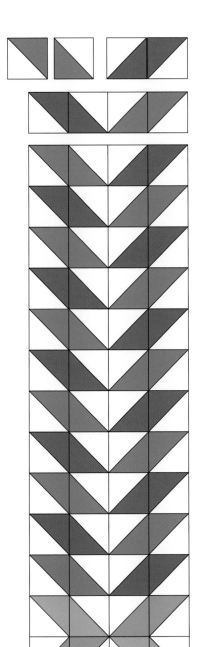
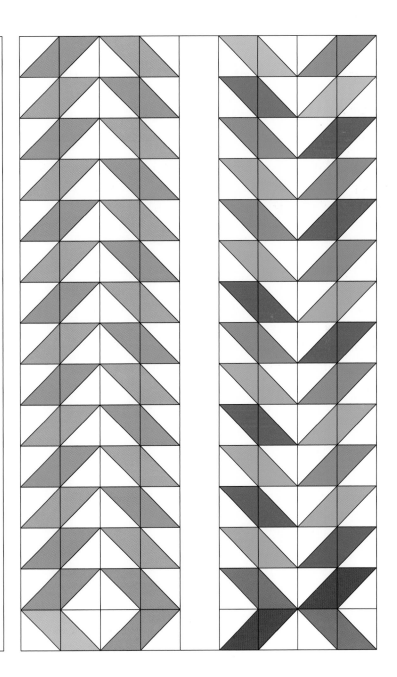

Quilt assembly

# RECTANGLES
# SQUARED

FINISHED QUILT: 66½" × 66½"  •  FINISHED BLOCK: 9" × 9"

Here's a great quilt for a beginner who wants a geometric design without having to think too hard about fabric planning. It is very modern, with lots of negative space and modern colors.

Depending on where the color change occurs within the block, this block could take on lots of different looks.

When you combine two rectangles 2″ × 3½″, you get a 3½″ × 3½″ square. But watch how versatile this little rectangle can be. …

---

## Materials

- 234 various assorted scraps, each large enough to yield a rectangle 2″ × 3½″

- 3 yards of solid white for alternate blocks, inner border, and outer border

- 75″ × 75″ backing

- 75″ × 75″ batting

- ⅝ yard for binding

## Cutting

See *Options for Cutting Scraps (page 8).*

### Scraps

#### FOR EACH BLOCK:

- Cut 12 rectangles 2″ × 3½″ of 1 main color from multiple prints for each of the 13 blocks (156 total).

- Cut 6 rectangles 2″ × 3½″ of 1 contrasting color from multiple prints for each of the 13 blocks (78 total).

#### FOR BORDER:

- Cut 76 rectangles 2″ × 3½″ in assorted colors.

### White

- Cut 12 squares 9½″ × 9½″ for the alternate blocks.

- Cut 6 strips 4½″ × width of fabric for the inner border.

- Cut 7 strips 5½″ × width of fabric for the outer border.

> **Note:** The main colors are the colors of the outermost rectangles and the center 2 rectangles. The contrasting colors are the ones that surround the center 2 rectangles.

# Marking the Template or Ruler

1. Use a 3½″ × 3½″ square template (such as the 3½″ fast2cut Simple Square Template by C&T Publishing), or mark a 3½″ × 3½″ square on a corner of your rotary cutting ruler.

2. Lay the template or ruler wrong side up on your gridded cutting mat, with the left side at the beginning of the mat measurements (0″).

3. Tear off a piece of tape 3½″ long. (I use Tear-Perfect Maker Tape by C&T Publishing.)

4. Place the edge of the tape, sticky side down, on the 2″ line.

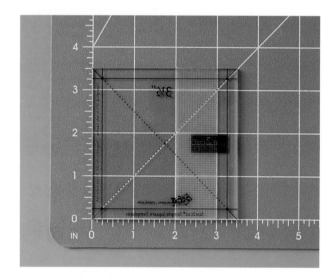

5. Flip the template over and you're ready to cut perfect 2″ × 3½″ rectangles.

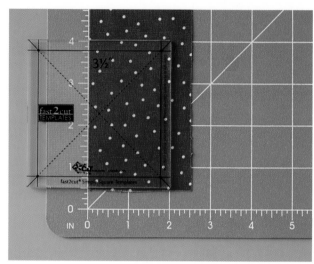

**TIP** *This quilt provides an absolutely perfect way to use up those old pieces left over from precut strip or precut square sets. There are always leftover pieces from those, and it's hard to know what to do with them.*

# Constructing the Quilt

*All seam allowances are ¼″. Follow the arrows for pressing directions.*

## Stitching the Blocks

1. Stitch 2 main-color rectangles together along the long sides.

2. Press the seam allowance toward the darker fabric.

3. Stitch a contrast-color rectangle to 2 opposite sides perpendicular to the center seam, as shown.

4. Press the seam allowances away from the center.

**5.** Stitch 2 contrast-color rectangles together along the short ends. Repeat this step to make a second unit.

**6.** Press the seam allowances to one side.

**7.** Stitch the contrast units to 2 opposite sides along the long edges, as shown.

**8.** Press the seam allowances toward the center.

**9.** Stitch 2 main-color rectangles together along the short ends. Repeat this step to make a second unit.

**10.** Press the seam allowances to one side.

**11.** Stitch the main-color units to 2 opposite sides, as shown.

**12.** Press the seam allowances toward the contrast-color rectangle.

**13.** Stitch together 3 main-color rectangles along the short ends. Repeat this step to make a second unit.

**14.** Press the seam allowances in the same direction.

**15.** Sew the main-color units to the contrast-color sides of the block.

**16.** Press the seam allowances toward the center.

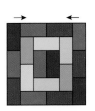

The basic block

**17.** Repeat Steps 1–16 to make a total of 13 blocks in different color combinations.

# Putting the Rows Together

1. Refer to the quilt assembly diagram (below) to lay out the pieced blocks and alternate squares in a 5 × 5 layout. Rotate alternating pieced blocks if desired.

2. Sew the blocks into rows. Press the seam allowances in each row in alternating directions.

3. Sew the rows together. Press.

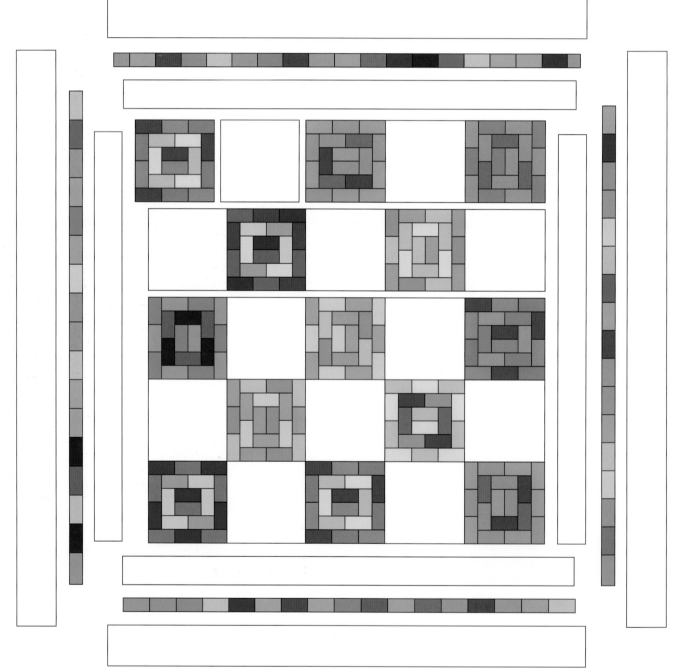

Quilt assembly

# Adding the Borders

## Inner Border

Follow How to Accurately Apply Borders (page 20) to add the inner border.

## Scrappy Border

**1.** Sew the 2″ × 3½″ rectangles together, right sides together and short end to short end, until there are 19 of them in a row. Repeat this step to make 4 total.

**2.** Follow How to Accurately Apply Borders (page 20) to add the scrappy border, trimming the borders to fit your measurements. For this quilt I applied the first border to the bottom of the quilt top and then worked counter-clockwise around the top.

## Outer Border

Follow How to Accurately Apply Borders (page 20) to add the outer border.

# Finishing

Layer, baste, quilt, and bind as desired.

# FRETWORK

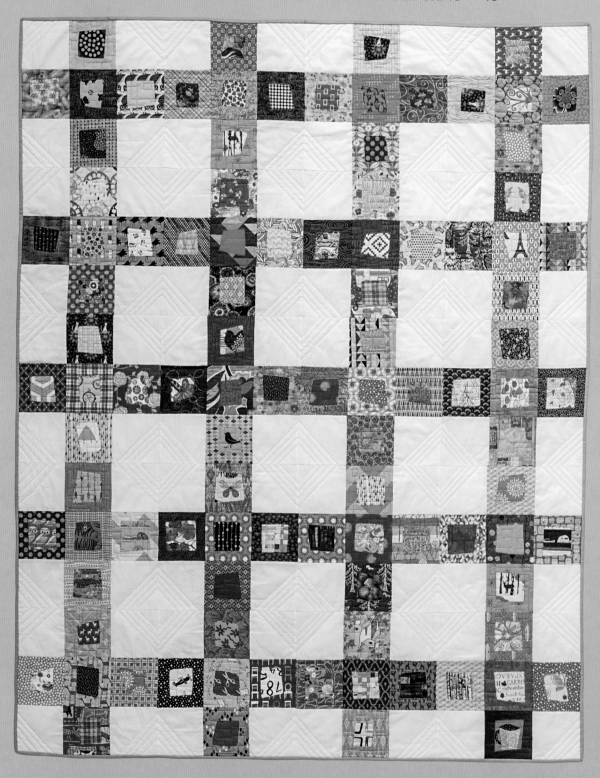

This quilt is actually reverse appliqué. It is such fun and uses up so many scraps. The best thing about it is how carefree it is.

The smaller squares inside the larger ones can be used to highlight something that deserves framing or something simple. Or it can place the emphasis on the fabric around the outside of the block.

This block is so easy that you will find yourself using it in other applications, such as pillows or table runners.

---

## Materials

- 100 assorted scraps, each large enough to yield a square 5½" × 5½"
- 100 assorted scraps, each large enough to yield a square 4½" × 4½"
- 2 yards of white for background blocks
- 69" × 84" backing
- 69" × 84" backing
- 5/8 yard for binding

## Cutting

See *Options for Cutting Scraps (page 8)*.

### Scraps

- Cut 100 squares 5½" × 5½".
- Cut 100 squares 4½" × 4½".

### White

- Cut 12 strips 5½" × width of fabric; subcut 80 squares 5½" × 5½".

---

# Making the Appliqué Units

*All seam allowances are ¼".*

**1.** Place a 5½" × 5½" scrap square wrong side up. Using a water-soluble pencil, mark a 3½" × 3½" square approximately in its center. (A 3½" × 3½" acrylic template, such as the 3½" fast2cut Simple Square Template from C&T Publishing, works very well for this.)

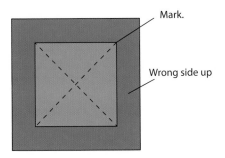

Mark.

Wrong side up

**2.** Using a rotary cutter, cut an X within the marked square.

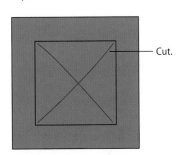

Cut.

**TIP** *It adds a lot of interest to cut the X's in a wonky fashion. This makes the shape of the openings much more fun.*

**3.** Pull the tips of the cut edges back, creating an opening in the square. Press.

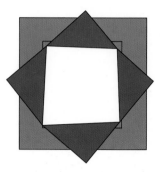

**TIP** *Make sure your iron is at the highest setting. The fabric needs to stay pulled back from the opening so that it is easier to stitch. You may also use spray starch to help it stay open.*

**4.** Turn the square right side up. Make sure that there are no raw edges showing on the edges of the opening.

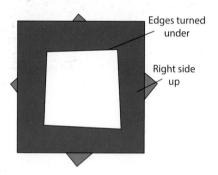

Edges turned under

Right side up

**TIPS**

• *It helps to take a wooden skewer or a toothpick and run it around the inner corner to keep any raw edge from poking out. As with the needle-turn appliqué technique, the wood helps to grab the fabric and keep it back.*

• *You can apply a single tiny drop of Fray Check to stabilize the corners.*

**5.** Place a 4½″ × 4½″ scrap square beneath the opening so that both fabrics are right side up, making sure the opening is completely covered and the fabric underneath is as close to the center as possible.

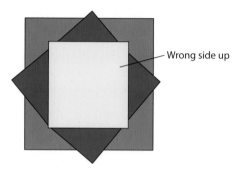

Wrong side up

**6.** From the right side, pin around the edge.

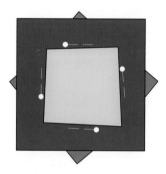

**7.** Stitch ¹⁄₁₆″ away from the edge all around the opening. Trim away the points of the pulled-back fabric.

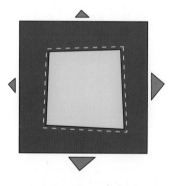

**8.** Repeat Steps 1–7 to make a total of 100 reverse appliqué units, 5 for each block.

# Assembling the Blocks

Each 15″ block is made up of the following:

  5 reverse appliqué units 5½″ × 5½″

  4 white squares 5½″ × 5½″

**1.** Lay out the reverse appliqué units and white squares as shown.

**2.** Join the units into rows. Press the seam allowances of each row in alternating directions: row 1 to the left, row 2 to the right, and row 3 to the left.

**3.** Sew the rows together. Press the seam allowances in one direction.

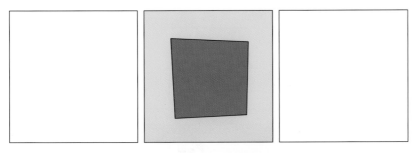

Block assembly

**4.** Repeat Steps 1–3 to make a total of 20 blocks.

# Putting It All Together

1. Lay out the blocks in a 4 × 5 layout.

2. Sew the blocks into rows. Press the seam allowances of each row in alternating directions.

3. Sew the rows together. Press the seam allowances in one direction.

# Finishing

Layer, baste, quilt, and bind as desired.

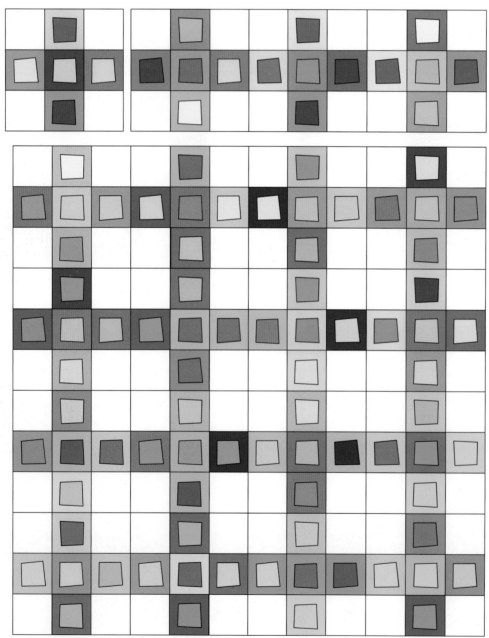

Quilt assembly

# ABOUT THE AUTHOR

Judy is the owner of Bungalow Quilting and Yarn, a modern quilt shop in Ripon, Wisconsin. She is also a fabric designer with Andover Fabrics.

A certified critical-care nurse, Judy holds a bachelor of science degree in nursing. She has 4 children and 2 grandchildren and has been married for 30 years. She resides in Ripon, Wisconsin, with her husband; Leroy, a standard poodle; Rico, the cockapoo; and 2 cats.

# Want even more creative content?

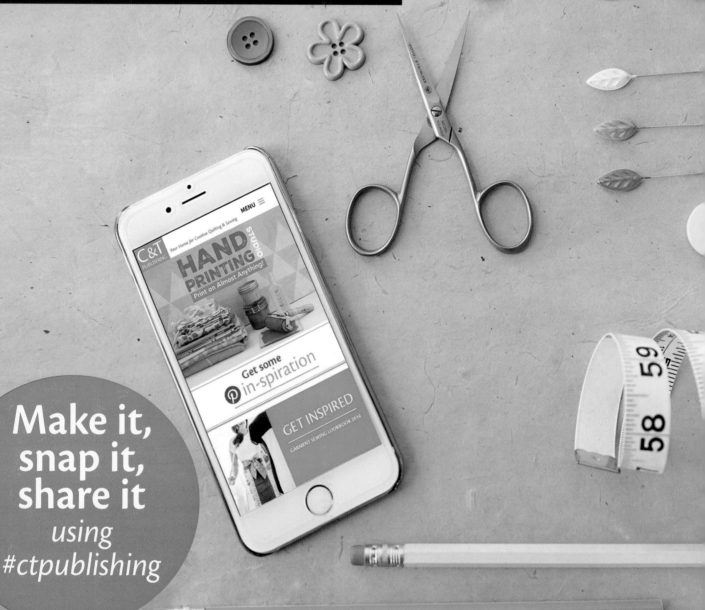

Make it, snap it, share it *using #ctpublishing*